REALISM, CARICATURE, AND BIAS

T0341373

THE LITTMAN LIBRARY OF
JEWISH CIVILIZATION

Dedicated to the memory of
LOUIS THOMAS SIDNEY LITTMAN
*who founded the Littman Library for the love of God
and as an act of charity in memory of his father*
JOSEPH AARON LITTMAN
and to the memory of
ROBERT JOSEPH LITTMAN
who continued what his father Louis had begun

יהא זכרם ברוך

'*Get wisdom, get understanding:
Forsake her not and she shall preserve thee*'

PROV. 4: 5

*The Littman Library of Jewish Civilization is a registered UK charity
Registered charity no.* 1000784

Realism, Caricature, and Bias

The Fiction of
Mendele Mocher Sefarim

◆

DAVID ABERBACH

London
The Littman Library of Jewish Civilization
in association with Liverpool University Press

The Littman Library of Jewish Civilization
Registered office: 4th floor, 7–10 Chandos Street, London W1G 9DQ

in association with Liverpool University Press
4 Cambridge Street, Liverpool L69 7ZU, UK
www.liverpooluniversitypress.co.uk/littman

Managing Editor: Connie Webber

Distributed in North America by
Oxford University Press Inc., 198 Madison Avenue,
New York, NY 10016, USA

First published in hardback and paperback 1993

Catalogue records for this book are available from the
British Library and the Library of Congress
ISBN 978-1-874774-08-2

Designed by Pete Russell, Faringdon, Oxon.

Printed and bound in Great Britain by
CPI Group (UK) Ltd., Croydon, CR0 4YY

To Moshe and Shoshana
with love and thanks

Acknowledgements

As a boy, I spent eight years at the Chofetz Chaim yeshivah in Baltimore, Maryland, and though not a very good student, I did gain an essential grounding in Talmud, mostly from eastern European rabbis who had come to the United States after the war, which has greatly enriched my reading of Mendele.

More immediately, I thank the British Academy and McGill University for research grants which facilitated the writing of this book.

I am grateful, too, to the librarians of the libraries which I used in the course of research: the National Library, Jerusalem; the Bodleian Library, Oxford; the School of Oriental and African Studies Library and the British Library, London; as well as the Kressel Archive, Yarnton Manor, Yarnton, Oxford, and Beit Tchernichovsky, Tel Aviv.

Among those who have helped and encouraged me in various ways over the years, I am thankful to the late Rabbi Dr David Goldstein and to Professors Samuel Werses, Abraham Nowersztern, and David Roskies. I also thank Professor Ruth R. Wisse and Dr Leon Yudkin, with whom I organized seminars on Mendele's Yiddish and Hebrew texts at McGill University, Montreal, and the Leo Baeck College, London, respectively. Not least, I am grateful to the late Louis Littman and to Colette Littman, as well as to Rabbi Dr Albert H. Friedlander and to Connie Wilsack, Publishing Editor of the Littman Library. Special mention must be made of Martin Gilbert, who very kindly compiled and drew the map of Mendele's world.

Finally, as always, I thank my wife Mimi, who has made this a work of joy and love.

Montreal, 1992   D.A.

Contents

Note on Transliteration

THE transliteration of Hebrew in this book reflects a consideration of the type of book it is, in terms of its content, purpose, and readership. The system adopted therefore reflects a broad approach to transcription, rather than the narrower approaches found in the *Encyclopedia Judaica* or other systems developed for text-based or linguistic studies. The aim has been to reflect pronunciation rather than spelling or word structure, and to do so using conventions that are generally familiar to the English-speaking Jewish reader. The pronunciation followed is that prescribed for modern Hebrew, on the grounds that this is what most readers will be familiar with: thus *tzitzit* is used in preference to *tzitzis*.

In accordance with this approach, no attempt is made to indicate the distinctions between *aleph* and *ayin*, *tet* and *taf*, *kaf* and *kuf*, *sin* and *samech*, since these are not relevant to pronunciation; likewise, the *dagesh* is not indicated except where it affects pronunciation. Following the principle of using conventions familiar to the majority of readers, however, transcriptions that are well established (for example, *kaddish*, *tallit*, *tefillin*—all of which, perhaps not by coincidence, belong to the world of Jewish ritual) have been retained even when they are not fully consistent with the transliteration system adopted. Similarly, the distinction between *chet* and *khaf* has generally been retained, using *ch* for the former and *kh* for the latter; the associated forms are generally familiar to readers, even if the distinction is not actually borne out in pronunciation. An important exception is in the name of Mendele himself: the form Mendele Mocher Sefarim is well established, and has therefore been retained. Familiar forms of personal names have likewise been retained in other instances, for example for Sholom Aleichem and Ahad Ha'am.

Since no distinction is made between *aleph* and *ayin*, they are indicated by an apostrophe only in intervocalic positions where a failure to do so could lead an English reader to pronounce the vowel cluster as a diphthong—as for example in *pe'ah*—or otherwise mispronounce the word. Here too, an allowance has been made for convention: *Yisrael* has been left as it is, without an apostrophe, since interference in this familiar form would constitute an intrusive intervention of no benefit to readers.

The *sheva na* is indicated by an *e*—*peleitah*, *berit*—except, again, when established convention dictates otherwise.

The *yod* is represented by an *i* when it occurs as a vowel (*maskilim*), by a *y* when it occurs as a consonant (*yonekim*), and by *yi* when it occurs as both (*yisrael*).

As an aid to pronunciation, a *tzeireh* at the end of a word is indicated by é. The *heh* at the end of words is indicated by an '*h*' even though it has no bearing on pronunciation, simply because this usage is widespread and therefore familiar.

The transliteration of Yiddish follows conventional practices that should be familiar to most readers.

Lower-case letters are used in all transliterations, except for the initial letter of titles and subtitles and proper names.

The World of Mendele Mocher Sefarim

St. Petersburg
son active in, as a revolutionary

Baltic Sea

TSARIST RUSSIA

LITHUANIA

Vilna
visited as a teenager

WHITE
RUSSIA

Kopyl
birthplace, about 1835

Timkovichi
lived after his father's
death in 1848

Slutsk
studied for two years

Warsaw

Lutsk
visited as a teenager

VOLHYNIA

POLAND

Kiev
Jews expelled, 1835

Lodz
visited, 1909

Kamenets-Podolsk
lived, 1852-58

Zhitomir
lived, 1869-81

UKRAINE

Berdichev
lived, 1858-69

THE PALE OF
SETTLEMENT

Sea
of Azov

—·—· Western borders of
Tsarist Russia 1815-1914

········ The border of the
Pale of Settlement

Odessa
lived, 1881-1917
died, 1917

CRIMEA

0   miles   200

0   kilometres   300

Black   Sea

© Martin Gilbert 1991

Introduction

FOR over 120 years until the Russian revolution of 1917, the Russian Jews, comprising nearly half of world Jewry, were confined by law in a closed area (the so-called Pale of Settlement) in the western part of the tsarist empire. They had come under Russian rule with the partitions of Poland in the late eighteenth century. Russia had not previously allowed Jews in, but had reluctantly accepted them as part of its conquests. The Jews had as little desire to be under tsarist rule, which was undisguisedly antisemitic, as the Russian government had to administer this strange and perplexing Yiddish-speaking, orthodox Jewish minority. A brief period of reform in the mid-nineteenth century (not unlike the *perestroika* of more recent years) led to reaction, and the pogroms of 1881–4 put an end to Jewish hopes of obtaining civil rights and emancipation under tsarist rule. This shattering of illusion was among the main forces leading to the rise of Jewish nationalism and thriving Yiddish and Hebrew literatures.

The most interesting and important Jewish novelist of the time was Mendele Mocher Sefarim (real name Shalom Ya'akov Abramowitz, 1835?–1917), whose works in both Yiddish and Hebrew give an unparalleled view of the psychological effects upon the Russian Jews of antisemitic prejudice and discrimination: of being largely unwanted second-class citizens, driven by tsarist rule to escape their impoverished condition through emigration, socialism, Zionism, or revolution. Mendele was in fact the most influential Jewish novelist prior to the destruction of European Jewry in the Second World War. He ranks among the chief literary ancestors of Sholom Aleichem and Isaac Bashevis Singer in Yiddish and of Samuel Joseph Agnon and Amos Oz in Hebrew.

Though the virtuosity of Mendele's style, especially in Hebrew, is hard to appreciate nowadays without close study not only of his works but also of his literary sources, the adulation which he aroused was not dissimilar from that of a film star today. On a tour of eastern Europe in 1909, he was feted everywhere; in the Polish town of Lodz, surrounded by thousands of admirers blocking the road, he suddenly felt his carriage lifted high above the heads of the crowd, and a deafening cry went up, 'Long live Mendele!'[1] When he died in Odessa shortly after the Bolshevik revolution, about fifty thousand people swarmed to his funeral, and his coffin was passed from hand to hand through the thick crowd until it reached the grave.

And yet, although loved to an extent virtually unknown among Jewish writers before or since, Mendele was a mordant critic of Jewish life. He portrayed not the moral grandeur of the East European Jews as much as their degradation and corruption. 'Two hate the Jews,' he once remarked to Chaim Chernowitz, chief rabbi of Odessa, 'the Lord on high and myself on earth.'[2] Not surprisingly, in the post-Holocaust years Mendele was attacked scathingly for accepting the antisemitic image of the Jews which prevailed in European culture.[3] Not infrequently, he draws on the crude clichés of antisemitism: the dirty, hook-nosed, uncouth, unproductive, devious Jew, smelling of onions and garlic, worshipping money. One would hardly guess that the Jews whom he describes belonged to the most dynamic and creative Jewish community of their time—that in the Russian Pale of Settlement.

Within the Zionist movement, Mendele's position was equally ambivalent. His depiction of the vile, ludicrous character of diaspora Jews could be, and often was, taken as an implicit rejection of the *galut* (exile), signifying the need to build a new life in the Land of Israel.[4] Yet he was not a political Zionist. Though he empathized with the Jewish pioneers in Palestine, he, in common with many Jews at the turn of the century, did not take seriously the notion of the mass return to the Land of Israel. His novella, *The Travels of Benjamin the Third*, is a classic satire on the idea of *aliyah* in which two absurd *shtetl* characters, Benjamin and Senderel, abandon their families and set out on foot for Eretz Yisrael. Mendele was at root an assimilationist who believed, even after the pogroms of 1881–4 and 1903–6, that the future of the Russian Jews lay in Russia.

[1] Related by David Frischmann, 'Mendele Mocher Sefarim', Introd. to *Kol kitvei Mendele Mocher Sefarim* (Collected Works of Mendele Mocher Sefarim), 3-vol. edn., vol. ii (Odessa, 1911), p. xxix.

[2] Rav Tzair [Chaim Chernowitz], *Masekhet zikhronot* (Memoirs), (New York, 1945), 22.

[3] See esp. Abraham Kariv, *Atarah leyoshenah* (Essays), (Tel Aviv, 1956). A comprehensive reply to Kariv and other critics of Mendele is given by Abba Haramati, *Bedikat hakitrug al Mendele* (An Investigation of the Criticism on Mendele), (Tel Aviv, 1984).

[4] Cf. Joseph Chaim Brenner, 'Ha'arakhat atzmeinu bisheloshet hakerakhim' (Our Self-Assessment in the Three Volumes [of Mendele's *Collected Works*, 1909–1912]), 1914, in *Kol kitvei J. C. Brenner* (Collected Works), vol. iii (Tel Aviv, 1967), 57–78.

For all the controversy surrounding Mendele, his reputation is secure: he is the first true artist and the shaping spirit both in Yiddish and modern Hebrew.[5] Sholom Aleichem called him the grandfather of modern Yiddish literature; to Bialik, he was the seminal figure of modern Hebrew prose style. His importance in modern Jewish literature is comparable with that of Sterne in English or Gogol in Russian. The first outstanding character in modern Jewish fiction, Mendele the Bookpeddler, was his creation, and he took this name as his own pseudonym.[6]

The character of Mendele recalls Chaplin's tramp in his combination of pathos and laughter.[7] Wandering through the Pale of Settlement, Mendele (the character as well as the author) observes his people with bitter affection, for though they are humiliated, they preserve traces of former nobility. In Mendele's hard-hitting satire *The Mare*, the Jews are depicted allegorically as a prince transformed by persecution and misfortune into a battered mare.

Most of Mendele's best-known work was first written in Yiddish, then reworked (not merely translated) into Hebrew. While his Yiddish has the ease, the colour, and the subtlety of the vernacular, his Hebrew is highly literary, though not artificial. Drawing heavily on biblical and rabbinic sources, he forged a style brilliant in its satiric depictions of the less fortunate elements in Russian Jewish society— the beggars, cripples, and misfits.

Together with a gallery of Breughel-like portraits, Mendele gives a wrenching account of the debilitating conditions which drove some two million Russian Jews to the United States, England, Palestine, and elsewhere at the turn of the century. Likewise, he has left a unique literary record of the effects of the pogroms of 1881–4, the demoralization, the sense of being unwanted, disoriented, isolated, not fully human. In Mendele's writings we have a world on the verge of destruction.

Mendele's life, which followed the sad, twisted course of Russian

[5] For a selected bibliography of works by and about Mendele, see the Bibliography, pp. 115–22. A survey of critical literature on Mendele is given by Samuel Werses in *Bikoret habikoret* (Criticism on Criticism), (Tel Aviv, 1982), 34–83.

[6] On the creation of the character of Mendele the Bookpeddler in the context of 19th cent. Yiddish fiction, see Dan Miron, *A Traveler Disguised* (New York, 1973). On the creation of Mendele's Hebrew style in the context of modern Hebrew prose fiction see Robert Alter, *The Invention of Hebrew Prose: Modern Fiction and the Language of Realism* (Seattle, 1988).

[7] The comparison between Mendele and Chaplin is elaborated upon in ch. 2 below.

Jewish history, casts light on the ambivalence towards the Jews in his art.[8] Born in the Lithuanian village of Kopyl (Kapuli) he grew up during the tyrannical reign of Nicholas I (1825–55). Like most Russian Jewish families at the time, Mendele's family was strictly observant. His father, Reb Chaim, dour, sickly, scholarly, was a communal leader and a collector of the meat-tax for the Russian authorities. Mendele's portrait of his father in *Of Bygone Days* is invariably respectful, even admiring, yet he has nothing but contempt for communal leaders and especially meat-tax collectors, whom he attacks viciously and frequently in his satires. The tax collectors were common targets in nineteenth-century Hebrew and Yiddish satire, and with good reason, as the historian Simon Dubnow explains: 'The tax situation became the worst plague in Jewish communal life. The tax collectors of the local plutocrats lorded over and fleeced the poor Jewish masses. This yoke brought about a demoralization in Jewish life.'[9] Relatively well educated both in religious and secular matters, Reb Chaim had status and influence as well as enemies. Mendele was apparently his favourite among at least five children.[10] He taught his son personally in the expectation that with his outstanding intellect he would become a great rabbi, and raised him to feel socially and intellectually a cut above the other Kopyl Jews. While Reb Chaim is clearly delineated in Mendele's autobiographical writings, his mother and siblings are not, and little is known of them.

Mendele's loss of his father in 1848, when he was just 13 or 14, was a blow from which he never fully recovered and whose effects fill his writings, particularly *Of Bygone Days* and *In the Valley of Tears*. This loss underlies his perception of the Jews as fallen aristocrats and of Jewish authority figures as untrustworthy and corrupt. It caused the break-up of his family, for his mother was unable to support them on her own. The status which the family had enjoyed while Reb Chaim was alive now vanished. Mendele spent the next few years wandering through the Pale, studying at various *yeshivot*, often living from hand to mouth. These wanderings were crucial to his later works, notably *The Travels of Benjamin the Third* and *The Beggar Book*. At one point, after his

---

[8] The fullest biography of Mendele to date is that of Joseph Klausner in vol. vi of *Historia shel hasifrut ha'ivrit hachadashah* (History of Modern Hebrew Literature), (Jerusalem, 1958). Further biographical sources are given in the Bibliography below.

[9] Simon Dubnow, *History of the Jews*, tr. M. Spiegel, vol. v (New York, 1973), 174–5.

[10] On Mendele's family background, see Max Weinreich, 'Mendeles eltern un mitkinder' (Mendele's Parents and Siblings), *YIVO Bleter*, 11 (1937), 270–86.

mother remarried, he came back to live with her and his step-father. Depressed, he began to write poetry and satire;[11] but soon he took to the road again and for several months lived virtually as a beggar, absorbing in his bones the worst in Jewish life.

After training as a teacher in Kamenets-Podolsk, he lived in Berdichev, one of the most depressed towns in Europe, a hell-hole of unemployment, overcrowding, and semi-starvation. Though he himself lived in relative comfort for most of his time in Berdichev and, later, in Zhitomir and Odessa, where he spent the latter half of his life as headmaster of a Jewish school with a modern orientation, he could not help but regard the Jews collectively as beggars and himself as an indigent 'Jew of Jews'.[12]

His world-outlook was further distorted by personal tragedies additional to the death of his father and the impoverishment and break-up of his family. In particular, there was the mental illness of his first wife, which forced him to divorce her in 1856; and the deaths of their two children around the same time (he remarried in 1858). Later, in the 1870s and 1880s, there were other griefs: the death of a beloved daughter, Rachel; and the exile of his only son, Michael (Meir), to Siberia, following activity in the revolutionary movement as a student in St Petersburg, and his eventual conversion to Christianity.

Until the pogroms, and especially during the reforms of Alexander II (1855–81), Mendele passionately hoped that by means of education and enlightenment achieved as a result of the Haskalah movement the Russian Jews would be granted civil rights and emancipation. The Jews might originally have been unwanted in Russia, but by learning the Russian language (a language which few Jews knew properly, even by the end of the nineteenth century) the Jews would gradually be accepted and integrated into Russian society—so Mendele and other Jewish intellectuals believed.

To further this aim, Mendele devoted himself prior to 1881 not to fiction but to educational textbooks, notably a three-volume *Natural History* in Hebrew, as well as polemical works calling for social reform—in this he was influenced by Russian writers such as Belinsky, Pisarev, and Turgenev. The spirit of reform which animates his early

---

[11] See *Kol kitvei Mendele Mocher Sefarim* (Collected Works of Mendele Mocher Sefarim), 1 vol. edn. (Tel Aviv, 1947), 3. Mendele kept these early works but never published them, and they disappeared after his death. The circumstances in which Mendele began to write are discussed in ch. 5.

[12] Ibid.; quoted p. 40 below.

works was universalistic in tone. Mendele was a pioneer in such causes as women's rights, improvements in the raising and education of children, and the humane treatment of animals.

An adverse effect of his work in social reform is summed up in one of his stories: 'No creature on earth is more miserable than Jews who think. They feel the hump on their back and are ashamed.'[13] There was an especial torture in belonging to a small group of enlightened Jewish intellectuals alienated to varying degrees from the wider Jewish community, yet not fully accepted in any stratum of Russian society.

Censorship, in addition, made it impossible openly to blame the Russian government for its discriminatory laws against the Jews (these filled a fat volume), for the existence of the Pale and the economic hardships which the Jews suffered in consequence. If anyone was to be blamed, it was the Jews themselves—with all the more bitterness and distortion as the outrage had to go somewhere. Mendele's stories have no Christian villains.

The pogroms of 1881–4 were a massive blow which changed Mendele's life. He gave up his educational writings and immersed himself in his fiction—Hebrew in particular. This was not just a response to the new market which opened with the rise of Zionism during and after the pogroms: it was an indirect declaration of independence, part of a growing wave of Jewish national feeling. Mendele's concentration on Hebrew was to continue for his last thirty years.

Paradoxically, though Mendele's subject was mainly the backwardness, the indignity, and the suffering of the Jews, the perfection of his art gave his people a sense of dignity and national pride. Perhaps for this reason few satirists have been as much loved as Mendele. By holding up a mirror to his people—however distorting the mirror was in places—he helped them to repair their shattered image.

Mendele retained his pre-eminent position in Jewish literature until

---

[13] *Kol kitvei*, 412. This poor self-image was exacerbated by the generally low opinion which enlightened Russians held of their own country. The disgust and condescension often felt by educated Russians towards the peasants is well expressed in Dostoyevsky's *Crime and Punishment* (1865–6), set shortly after the liberation of the serfs in 1861. The examining magistrate Porphiry jokes sardonically with Raskolnikov that no educated murderer would take refuge in the Russian countryside: 'Our modern educated Russian would sooner be in jail than live among such foreigners as our peasants'. Tr. D. Magarshak, Penguin edn. (Harmondsworth, Middx., 1966), 355.

the Second World War. Since then he has had the dual misfortune of losing his Yiddish readers and of being superseded in Hebrew. His writings deserve a better destiny: not only do they provide a record of the turbulent life of the Russian Jews under the tsars, but by chronicling human resilience in exceptionally damaging conditions, they give insight into the lives of the majority of the world's population today. They remind us, as do the works of Dickens and Tolstoy, how recently the West has emerged from conditions that today are associated with the Third World.

This book explores some of the conflicting strands of realism and caricature in Mendele's fiction, interpreting them partly in the context of nineteenth-century Russian social and literary history but mainly in psychological terms. Mendele's satires of the Jews and of himself are seen to run parallel to one another: his portrayal of the Jews is virtually a self-portrait. Full-length critical studies have been devoted to many aspects of Mendele's works,[14] but this approach has been largely neglected.

Few writers have had such strongly conflicting views of their people as Mendele, or aroused such passionate extremes of love and hatred. His full pen-name, Mendele Yudelevich (used only in *Dos kleyne mentschele*, though not in the first version, of 1864–5), roughly translated 'little man, son of a Jew', purposefully belies the scope of his achievement and the universality of his appeal. He is a writer of many voices, some of which have faded with time, but the chief voices, those of the realist and the satirist, still entertain and enlighten. Mendele's complexity is heightened by the variety of differences in the Yiddish and Hebrew versions as well as by the subtle, often ironic interplay between Mendele the literary figure and his creator, S. Y. Abramowitz. The two are superficially dissimilar but have much in common, particularly in psychological make-up. These aspects of Mendele's art are discussed in the opening chapters as part of the general theme of conflict between realism and bias. They lead to an analysis of further elements of Jewish self-hate, of social and psychological realism as well as the struggle for a new identity and self-definition through Haskalah. An ensuing exploration of autobiography in Mendele leads to a conclusion which interprets the origins of bias in his works in the light of his own family history and experience.

[14] See the Bibliography.

A NOTE ON TEXTS

Practically all Mendele's major fiction was written both in Yiddish and in Hebrew. While a limited comparison between the Yiddish and Hebrew drafts is made in Chapter 1, this book is mainly about the content, which is largely identical in the two languages. Unless indicated otherwise, quotations are from the Hebrew final drafts in the one-volume *Kol kitvei Mendele Mocher Sefarim* (Collected Works), (Tel Aviv, 1947), based on the 1909–12 three-volume edition. The contents of this volume, with details of the publishing history of the various works, are as given below. The principal source for the latter is Samuel Werses and Chone Shmeruk (eds.), *Mendele Mocher Sefarim: Bibliography of his Works and Letters for the Academic Edition* (Jerusalem, 1965).

1. 'Reshimot letoledotai' ('Autobiographical Notes'), 1899. No Yiddish draft.

2. *Ha'avot vehabanim* (Fathers and Sons), 1868, 1912. No Yiddish draft.

3. *Masot Binyamin Hashelishi* (The Travels of Benjamin the Third). Yiddish 1878, Hebrew 1896.

4. *Sefer hakabtzanim* (The Beggar Book), 1909. Yiddish drafts, under the title *Fishke der Krummer* (Fishke the Lame), 1869, 1888.

5. *Be'emek habakhah* (In the Valley of Tears), 1896–1908. Yiddish drafts, under the title *Dos vinshfingerl* (The Magic Ring), 1865, 1889, 1913.

6. *Bayamim hahem* (Of Bygone Days), 1903–10, 1917. The Introduction appeared in 1894. Yiddish version, under the title *Shloyme Reb Chayims* (Shloyme, Son of Reb Chayim), 1899, 1912–13, 1917.

7. *Susati* (The Mare), 1911. Yiddish drafts, under the title *Die kliatsche* (The Mare), 1873, 1888, 1911.

8. *Sefer habehemot* (The Beast Book):
   —'Eglato shel Tosafot Yom Tov' (The Calf), Yiddish 1910, Hebrew 1911.
   —'Lekorot sus nosé sefarim' (History of a Book-Carrying Horse), Yiddish 1902, Hebrew 1911.

9. *Misefer hazikhronot* (The Memory Book). Pt. 1: Yiddish 1913, Hebrew 1915; pt. 2: Yiddish and Hebrew, 1915.

10. *Sipurim ketanim* (Short Stories):
    —'Beseter ra'am' (Shelter from the Storm), 1886–7*
    —'Lo nachat beYa'akov' (No Peace for Jacob), Hebrew 1892, Yiddish 1895
    —'Shem veYefet ba'agalah' (Shem and Japheth in the Train), 1890
    —'Biyemei hara'ash' (Earthquake Days), 1894*
    —'Biyeshivah shel ma'alah uviyeshivah shel matah' (Warsaw 1881), 1894–5*
    —'Hanisrafim' (The Fire Victims), Hebrew 1897, Yiddish 1900

11. *Chagim uzemanim* (Festivals):
    —'Chag ha'asif' (Festival of Gathering), Hebrew 1904, Yiddish 1909
    —'Mai Chanukah?' (What is Chanukah?), Hebrew 1912*
    —'Hatemurah' (The Exchange), Hebrew 1912*
    —'Hasa'arah' (The Hair), Hebrew and Yiddish 1905
    —'Leyom hashabbat' (For the Sabbath), Hebrew 1911

References throughout are to the English titles as given above.

The sole major piece of Yiddish fiction which Mendele did not rework into Hebrew was *Dos kleyne mentschele* (1864–5, 1879, 1907), referred to as *The Parasite*, the title of its English translation by Gerald Stillman.

Translations are my own unless indicated otherwise. Further information on Mendele's writings is given in the Bibliography.

Mendele gave the towns in which his Jews lived names that expressed his conception of these towns, as will be clear from the following comparison:

Yiddish	*Hebrew*	*English*
Tuniadevka	Batlon	Idlerstown
Glupsk	Kesalon	Foolstown
Kabtsansk	Kabtziel	Beggarville

The pen-name Mendele is used to identify the author except in Chapter 2, where the name Abramowitz is used.

---

* Yiddish versions of these stories were prepared by, or in collaboration with, a translator for the 1911–13 edition of Mendele's collected Yiddish works.

I

The Five Twice-Told Novels

MENDELE wrote five of his novels in two languages: first Yiddish, then Hebrew. The various drafts gain in fascination when read in tandem and compared: they give insight into Mendele's motives and achievement, revealing that he did not just translate but recast the Yiddish. While the sense is the same, the literary effects of the Hebrew are often totally different from those of the Yiddish. As a Yiddish writer, Mendele belongs, as the mood takes him, to satiric, sentimental, realistic, and picaresque traditions, particularly of the Russian and English novel. As a Hebrew writer he breaks new ground in his use of the classical sources, his manipulation of a parallel between present and past. In this respect, he anticipates modernists such as Joyce and Eliot.

Mendele was by far the most remarkable of the bilingual writers of his age, though most nineteenth and early twentieth-century Yiddish writers also wrote in Hebrew, and vice versa: these included Y. L. Peretz and Sholom Aleichem, Bialik and Agnon. The phenomenon of a writer writing the *same* work both in Yiddish and in Hebrew had existed from the early nineteenth century—perhaps the best example is that of Joseph Perl's anti-hasidic satire *Megaleh temirin* (Revealer of secrets, 1819). The heyday of this phenomenon was in the period 1881–1914, from the outbreak of the pogroms until the start of the First World War. This was a time of social and religious breakdown and reorganization, when the majority of Jews were still Yiddish speakers, but as the Zionist movement grew, an increasing number read and spoke modern Hebrew. During this period, Mendele rewrote in Hebrew five of his six major Yiddish works: *The Mare, The Travels of Benjamin the Third, The Beggar Book, In the Valley of Tears*, and *Of Bygone Days*.

Implicit in the two versions are the different roles and status of Yiddish and Hebrew in the traditional life of the east European Jews. Yiddish was a practical, everyday, and highly expressive language which had flourished continuously since the Middle Ages. Still, it was commonly despised by educated Jews and Gentiles as a language unfit to be a vehicle for modern education, being as they wrongly saw it a grotesque hybrid of German, Hebrew and other languages. (Since the Holocaust and the largely successful attempt to destroy Yiddish and its speakers totally, there has been a reaction in the opposite direction, and this makes it all the more difficult to appreciate the hostility which Yiddish once aroused, even among its writers.) Hebrew, in contrast, had been used since rabbinic times for prayer and study and was venerated by non-Jews as well as Jews, if not as the Holy Tongue then at least as a great classical language. For this reason, of the two languages with which East European Jews were most familiar, Hebrew seemed logically the best one to serve them, initially at least, as a means of exposure to modern life, to science, and to art. And so, from the late eighteenth century onwards, secular Hebrew literature had developed, with limited success, mainly as a didactic tool used to introduce the largely uneducated European Jews to secular enlightenment. An outstanding example of this type of writing, as we have seen in the *Introduction*, was Mendele's own *Natural History* which was aimed mainly at Jews thirsting for an education in the sciences who could not read German science textbooks but could read Hebrew.

These differences in usage between Yiddish and Hebrew are reflected in Mendele's style. His Yiddish stories may be read easily, as straightforward, highly colloquial literature, whereas the Hebrew reworkings demand close study as they allude constantly to biblical, rabbinic, and medieval sources—allusions which are mostly absent in the Yiddish. These sources are played off, often with brilliant success, against the world which they are employed to describe: the poverty and degradation of Jewish life in the Pale of Settlement. (This play is found also in the Yiddish, which has a substantial Hebrew vocabulary, but not to the same extent, or as successfully, as in the Hebrew texts.) Mendele's most enduring achievement—illustrated later in this chapter—was to give modern Hebrew literary prose the breath of life via Yiddish. By drawing on the full associative richness of the Hebrew sources, he created a supple and highly original style. In doing so, he gave devastating, unprecedented expression to the powerful, often ironic clash between the spiritual ideals of Judaism and the shocking material realities which seemed to make a mockery of these ideals. It may be that only through Yiddish could Mendele succeed as he did with Hebrew: only by first raising Yiddish from its status as a contemptible 'jargon' to that of a great literary language was he later able, by building on the Yiddish model, to expand the status of Hebrew from Holy Tongue to a vehicle for serious secular literature.

Just as the two languages betray a split self-image within the Jewish people, so also they bring out a parallel ambivalence in the author's self-image. During the first half of his career, Mendele had in effect two separate careers, in Yiddish and in Hebrew, under two different names. From 1857, when his first Hebrew article appeared, until 1886–7, with the publication of his Hebrew short story 'Shelter from the Storm', all his Hebrew prose was signed 'S. Y. Abramowitz'. During this time, he also wrote a number of Yiddish novels, in which the name 'Abramowitz' is absent but which, in the author's playful fiction, were written by one or another of the characters and rewritten and published by the fictional Mendele. In his 'Autobiographical Notes' (4–5), the author implicitly compares this authorial split to simultaneous affairs with two women: Hebrew was his faithful, loving wife, while Yiddish was his mistress, whom he visited furtively under a false name, and who mothered his illegitimate children. Only after the pogroms of 1881–4, in 'Shelter from the Storm', did Mendele first appear in a *Hebrew* story. This seemingly innocuous act was symbolically momentous, both in the author's career and in the history of modern Hebrew literature. It marked the point when Yiddish sensibility entered Hebrew fiction and brought it to life as art. At this time, too, Sholom Aleichem's affectionate use of the name Mendele to describe the author as well as the character he created began to catch on. By the mid-1890s, the character of Mendele was so closely associated with Abramowitz that from then on he was universally known as Mendele.

After experimenting successfully from 1886 onward with a series of Hebrew stories, Mendele began in the mid-1890s to rewrite his Yiddish novels in Hebrew. Both versions were written in the knowledge that either language or both might be largely forgotten within a few generations. Though Mendele was passionately devoted to Hebrew, his rewritings also reflect a cool appraisal of his chances of being read in Yiddish by future generations. These Hebrew works comprise in effect an insurance policy with the future, a hedging of bets against oblivion. Mendele is still in danger of falling into the trap of oblivion which threatens writers whom everyone praises and no one reads. His subtlety, wit, and intelligence are such that he is best read in the original texts. But Mendele's Yiddish and Hebrew are not easy and, in addition, the world which he describes is foreign to the modern reader. For these reasons, there cannot be many writers whose genius is so hard to appreciate as Mendele's.

The following discussion of texts from the five twice-written novels serves as a thumbnail sketch of this achievement. By comparing the two versions, the reader can gain a clear picture of Mendele's methods, his style in each language, and some elements of the caricature and bias which are analysed in later chapters. In each case, an English translation is followed by its Yiddish original, then by the Hebrew reworking of the Yiddish, and finally by a discussion of the Hebrew.

I. *THE MARE*

And so, gentlemen, you merciful directors of our splendid Society, you, whose commiseration is so vast for all animals, all beasts, please take pity on the poor, wretched mare! Stand beside it in its misery and protect it against tribulations. Spread your wings over it and help it to salvation. Let the ill-fortuned creature know that the world is no longer an abandoned place! Today we have a Society for the Prevention of Cruelty to Animals![1]

און איהר, באַרמהאַרצעצדיגע גבאים פֿון דער טייערער חברה, וואָס אייער רחמנות איז אַזוֹי גרוֹיס אוֹיף אלע חיות, אוֹיף אלע בהמות, דערבאַרמט אייך אוֹיף דער וויסטער, אומגליקליכֿער קליאַטשע! שטעהט איהר בײַ אין איהרע נוֹיטען און נעהמט זיך אָן איהר קריוודע. שפרייעט אוֹיף איהר אוֹיס אייערע פֿליגעל און לאָז זי דוּרך אייך געהאָלפֿען ווערען. לאָז זי, שלימפמזלדיגע, נעבבעך, אוֹיף וויסען, אז היינטיגע צייט איז נישט מעהר הפֿקר אַ וועלט. עס איז דאָ אַ חברה "צער בעלי-החיים"! 2

ואתם, גבאים נכבדים, ראשי החברה, המתנהגים עם כל החיות ועם כל הבהמות במדת-הרחמים, יהמו נא רחמיכם גם על בריה זו, העלובה והשוממה! הצילו נפש נענה זו ועשו משפטה ודינה, תחסה תחת כנפיכם ותושע בכם ועל ידיכם תשועת עולמים. תדע עלובה זו אף היא, שעכשיו אין העולם הפקר ויש בו חברה "צער בעלי-חיים"! (329)

The first version of *The Mare* was written the year after the first Russian pogrom, which occurred in 1871 in Odessa. The Russian Jewish press was not allowed to mention the atrocities, and Mendele's novel was a thinly disguised *cri de cœur* of an enlightened Russian Jew

---

[1] Tr. Joachim Neugroschel in *Great Works of Jewish Fantasy* (London, 1976), 617–18.
[2] *Ale verk fun Mendele Mocher Sefarim* (Collected Works), (Warsaw etc., 1911–13 edn.), II. i. 100.

whose previous faith that Jewish emancipation was possible under tsarist rule was severely tested. In the novel, a young Jew named Israel, the only child of his widowed mother, is barred from entering medical school by antisemitic university examiners. Soon after, he suffers a breakdown in which he has his hallucinations of the mare— hallucinations that are eminently sane and filled with potent social satire. Among Mendele's targets are liberal societies such as the Society for the Promotion of Enlightenment among the Russian Jews —a society of which he (as Abramowitz) was a member and beneficiary—founded in St Petersburg in 1863 by a small group of wealthy and educated Jews in the belief that education and assimilation would earn the Jews civil rights and ultimate emancipation. Mendele mocks this society (and similar ones) as a Society for the Prevention of Cruelty to Animals, naïve and self-important, and lacking real power and influence. Israel, in fantasy a well-meaning member of this society, naïvely thinks that his influence can stop hooligans from hurting the mare. He drafts an appeal to the society, concluding with a flourish of false hope: 'Today we have a Society for the Prevention of Cruelty to Animals!'

The cutting edge of Mendele's satire in each version is aimed both at the Russian Jewish intellectuals who (like the author himself) clung to illusions, and also at the blind hatred that went against Russian interests. Animals had protection societies: the Jews did not. Animals could be hunted only at certain times of year: Jews were fair game at all times. The two voices in this passage—of Israel and of the author— clash as voices of innocence and experience, illusion and disillusion, hope and sarcasm.

The Yiddish version subtly and unselfconsciously catches a number of echoes from Scripture, the Talmud, and the liturgy which are pointedly amplified in the Hebrew. In particular, qualities associated in the sources with God, such as mercy (*rachmonus* = *rachmanut*—the same word in both languages), are attributed to the directors of the society, who are described in both languages as *gaba'im*, normally used in the sense of synagogue leaders. These men, by implication, have a semi-religious function, which they do not fulfil. The Yiddish *vos eier rachmonus iz azoy groys oyf ale chayes*, 'whose commiseration is so vast for all animals', is transformed into the Hebrew *hamitnahagim im kol hachayot ve'im kol habehemot bemidat harachamim*, 'who treat all animals and all beasts according to the quality of mercy'. The literal meanings of both phrases are virtually identical, but the echoes of the Hebrew convey an ingenious allusive reference to the talmudic speculation that God prays: 'May it be my will that my mercy will overcome my anger, and I will treat my sons according to the quality of mercy' (Ber. 7*a*). Similarly, the Yiddish *derbarmt eich*, 'take pity', is given in the Hebrew as *yehemu na rachamekhem*, which means practically the same thing, but with a difference: the phrase used is derived from the Amidah prayer, 'Towards the righteous . . . may your tender mercy be stirred [*yehemu na rachamekha*], O Lord our God.' This call for mercy directed at ineffectual human beings in language usually associated with a plea to the Almighty could suggest a heretical view that mercy is found neither with man nor with God.

Ironic references to God's mercy, power, and salvation continue in the following Hebrew sentences: the image of God (or of the *shekhinah*) spreading protective wings over his people is familiar from the prayer for the dead, *el malé rachamim*, and elsewhere; there is also a direct allusion to Isa. 45: 17, 'Israel is saved by the Lord with everlasting salvation', the mare's condition being a far cry from this. The dismissal of the idea that the world is 'an abandoned place' (*hefker*, in both languages) is a parody of a similar dismissal in the midrash (Lam. Rab. 1: 16)—except that the authorial voice in *The Mare*, here as elsewhere, twists the source round, for the author clearly believes or suspects that the world is, indeed, *hefker*.

2. *THE TRAVELS OF BENJAMIN THE THIRD*

This is Mendele the Bookpeddler speaking: Praised be the Creator Who fixes the destiny of the heavenly spheres and the fate of all His earthly creatures. Even the least blade of grass will not sprout unless some angel urge it on: Grow, now! Come forth! How much more so in the case of man, whom an angel most certainly must urge on: Grow on! Come forth! And still more with our praiseworthy little Jews. Among us no oaf dare open his mouth out of turn, a simpleton doesn't step into a sage's shoes, an ignoramus into a pietist's, a boor into a learned gentleman's, until such time as each oaf, simpleton, ignoramus and boor is goaded and urged on by some angel. It is likewise the angels who urge on our paupers of every sort, admonishing them: Grow, ye poor, ye beggars—beggars born, beggars broken-down, plain-spoken and close-mouthed—sprout, spring up like grass, like nettles! Go ye forth, ye Jewish children—go ye begging from door to door![3]

[3] Tr. Moshe Spiegel, *The Travels and Adventures of Benjamin the Third* (New York, 1949), 9.

אָמר מענדעלע מוכר־ספרים, זאָגט מענדעלע מוכר־ספרים, געלויבט איז דער בורא, וואָס
באַשטימט דעם גאַנג פֿון גלגלים אין די הימלען אויבן און דעם גאַנג פֿון זיינע אַלע
באַשעפֿענישן אויף דער ערד אונטן. אפֿילו אַ גרעזעלע קריכט נישט אַרויס פֿון דער ערד,
ביזוואַנען אַ מלאך שלאָגט עס נישט און זאָגט: וואַקס! קריך אַרויס! מכל־שכן אַ מענטש, ער
האָט אָודאַי אַ מלאך, וואָס שלאָגט אים און זאָגט: גיי, גיי, קריך אַרויס! און מכל־שכן נאָך מער
די פֿיינע מענטשעלעך, שיינע יידעלעך. — קיין נאַר כאַפּט זיך פֿריער פֿון איטלעטכן נישט אַרויס
מיט אַ וואָרט ביי אונדז, קיין שוטה ווערט נישט קיין בעל־עצה, קיין עם־הארץ — אַ חסיד, קיין
גראָבער יונג — אַ משכיל, ביזוואַנען אַ שלאָגט עס נישט איטלעטכן פֿון זיי זיין מלאך, נייטנדיק
אים דערצו. עס שלאָגן די מלאכים אויך אַלע מיני קבצנים אונדזערע, זאָגנדיק: וואַקסט,
קבצנים, אביונים, דלפֿנים, געבירעֿרענע, אָפּגעקומענע, אָפֿענע, פֿאַרבאַרגֿענע, שפּאראָצט, וואַקסט
ווי גראָז, ווי קראָפּעווע! גיט, יידישע קינדער, גיט — איבער די הייזער!⁴

אמר מנדלי מוכר־ספרים: יתברך הבורא וישתבח היוצר, שהוא מנהיג את הגלגלים בעולמות
העליונים ואת בריותיו בעולם התחתון ומבין לכל הליכותיהם. אין לך עשב שאין לו מלאך,
שמכהו ואומר לו: "גדל!" ואם עשב כך, קל־וחומר בן־אדם, וקל־וחומר בן־בנו של קל־וחומר
אדם מישראל. אין הדיוט קופץ בראש, אין שוטה נעשה פלא־יועץ, ואין עם־הארץ — חסיד
ובור — משכיל אצלנו, אלא עד שכל אחד ואחד מהם המלאך שלו מכהו וכופאו להיות מה
שהוא. אף קבצנינו, ארחי־פרחי שלנו, מלאכי־השרת מכים אותם ואומרים להם: "פרו־ורבו,
קבצנים! בית־יעקב, לכו — וחזרו על הפתחים!" (57)

The character of Mendele appears only once in the narratives of the
five twice-written novels, in *The Beggar Book*. However, with the exception of *The Beggar Book*, each of these novels has a preface by Mendele[5]
that among other things, explains with tongue-in-cheek his role in
obtaining the manuscript and editing it for publication. (The novel *The
Parasite* and the play *Die takse* (The Tax, 1869) also have introductions
of this sort by Mendele, making a total of six.) Taken together, these
prefaces comprise the most original writing in Mendele's *œuvre*: they
present the character of Mendele the Bookpeddler, they create the
satiric tone with great versatility and charm, and they state the thematic
ironies and contradictions which are developed in the narratives.

Two of the main satiric themes in Mendele, God's maltreatment of
his people and the alienation of the Jews from nature, appear in the
opening paragraph of the preface to *The Travels of Benjamin the Third*.
(Similar but less subtle openings appear also in *The Tax* and *In the
Valley of Tears*.[6]) Echoes from Psalms, 'he who fashions the hearts of

---

[4] *Ale verk*, VI, ii. 3–4. The 1878 version of this passage is substantially different,
though it conveys the same sense.

[5] The Introd. to *The Mare* appeared only in Yiddish, while that of *In the Valley of Tears*,
the most remarkable of the introductions, was published only in the original Hebrew
serial version.   [6] See Miron, *A Traveler Disguised*, 141 ff.

them all and observes all their deeds' (33: 15); from the Midrash, 'Rabbi Simeon said: "There is not a single blade of grass that does not have its guiding star in heaven which beats it, saying: Grow!"' (Gen. Rab. 10: 6); and from the medieval *nishmat* prayer, 'who guides his world with lovingkindness and his creatures with mercy' combine to create a tone of ecstatic faith in God's power and goodness, even in the knowledge of death (the verbs *yitbarakh*, blessed, and *yishtabach*, praised, are taken from the Kaddish, the mourner's doxology). Other allusions—for example to Isa. 9: 5, *Meg.* 12*b*, Ethics of the Fathers 2: 5, *Ket.* 61*a*—reinforce the mood of belief in providence firmly rooted in Scripture. And although a Yiddish-speaking angel urging a blade of grass to grow—*Krich aroys!*—is hard to take seriously, it does after all spring from a rabbinic source. But when the angels begin to urge Jewish beggars to sprout like grass and nettles—*Vakst, kabtzonim, evyoinim, dalfonim . . . vi groz, vi karpove*—the reader is whisked from synagogue to theatre, to a tragi-comic topsy-turvy world of farce. The destructive chaos which typified Jewish life in the Pale is expressed in the way Mendele's texts suddenly go haywire, and, in a frenzy of Mephistophelean mockery, devour the scriptural meat they feed on.

The first *mitzvah* (commandment) recorded in the Bible, 'Be fruitful and multiply' (Gen. 1: 24), which Mendele quotes in the Hebrew, *peru urevu*, was evidently not intended for overcrowded, unemployed, hungry paupers. The grand vision of Isaiah (2: 5) of the end of days, when all nations will stream to the House of the Lord and the Jews will be a light unto the nations, *beit Ya'akov lekhu venelekha be'or Adonai* (O House of Jacob, come, let us walk in the light of the Lord), is deflated with devastating mockery in Mendele's Hebrew, *beit Ya'akov, lekhu—vechizru al hapetachim* (O House of Jacob, go—begging from door to door). If this is providential will, the author will have none of it, for the passivity encouraged by such beliefs is dangerous.

In a few sentences, then, Mendele sets up a matrix whose satiric themes extend throughout the book, for the mock heroes, Benjamin and Senderel, are themselves roused by the angel of paupery to seek their fortunes begging further than at home.

3. *THE BEGGAR BOOK*

There, on the tables and benches, Kabbalists [students of the Zohar, the central text of Jewish mysticism] lay stretched out like princes and whistled to each other through their noses in all the tones of the scale. It was a pleasure to see, may the Evil Eye not harm them, how soundly they slept. Kabbalists really have it soft in the world, I thought, and in my heart I envied them. They are an altogether different type of beggar—somehow they're respectable.[7]

אין קליידזעל ליגען אויף טיש און אויף ביינק אויסגעצוינגען מקבלים און שלאָפען און די פריצים, איבערגעפייפענדיג זיך מיט נעז צוורישען זיך אויף אַלערליי קולות. אַ מחיה געווען צו זעהן, ווי געשמאַק, אָהן עין־הרע, זיי זענען געשלאָפען. מקבלים איז טאַקי אויף דער וועלט גוט, האָב איך מיר געטראַכט און זיי אין האַרצען מקנא געווען. דאָס זענען עפיס גאָר אַנדערע מיני קבצנים, נגידישע ...[8]

ובבית־המדרש שוכבים סרוחים בטלנים על ספסלים ושולחנות כבני מלכים וישנים, נוחרים זה לזה בנחיריהם וחוטם אל חוטם קורא בקולות משונים. אשרי עין — אמרתי, מתקנא בם — ראתה את אלה כשהם נרדמים בשלוה. אך טוב להבטלנים בעולם הזה. מי בקבצנים ידמה להם ומי ישוה להם! (128)

None of Mendele's novels offers so sharp a contrast with his earlier non-fiction as *The Beggar Book*. The stern, scientific, critical face of the educator is transformed into the Janus face of the satirist, mocking yet compassionate. One of the set pieces in *The Beggar Book* (114–15) is, in fact, a brilliant parody of the scientific method of exposition which he had used in his educational textbooks—a detailed classification of beggar species. In these textbooks, which were hardly read in his day let alone in ours, he promoted science as a means of social change, while apparently ignoring the misery of Jewish life in the Pale, for such works did nothing to alleviate it. The pogroms changed him: he gave up writing textbooks and, instead, portrayed in loving detail the lives of the poorest class of Jews in the Pale. The heart of *The Beggar Book* is no overt educational message but a love story of Fishke the cripple and Beila the hunchback, two unfortunates cast by chance among a wretched band of itinerant beggars. Dregs of society's dregs, outcasts among the outcasts, they are treated with undisguised contempt and hostility. In one scene, Fishke is savaged by one of the beggars and rescued by Beila. They seek refuge in the local synagogue, where a number of other tramps and beggars are already fast asleep.

Here again, the ironies of poverty are brought out, in relation to the squalid present in the Yiddish and in relation to the glorious past in the Hebrew. The Yiddish voice, using idiomatic expressions and constructions, such as *shlofn vi di poritzim* (sleeping like *poritzim*, a *poritz* being a gentile country squire who would often lord it over his

---

[7] Tr. Gerald Stillman, *Fishke the Lame* (New York, 1960), 161.
[8] *Ale verk*, II. ii. 136.

tenants—the English 'princes' is inaccurate here), *iberfeifendig sich mit nez* (whistling through the nose), *a mechaye* (a pleasure), *ohn ayin hora* (may the Evil Eye not harm them), *mekane geven* (I envied them), *nogidische* (noble-like), could be imagined as that of a poor, uneducated but intelligent and colourful beggar, which Fishke is. The irony is basic and transparently stated: these miserable specimens, sprawled exhausted in the house of worship, are an object of envy to Fishke: so low has he fallen that he admires and takes pleasure in the 'nobility' of these so-called Kabbalists, the comfort of their position, the soundness of their sleep (sleep is denied him), even the orchestration of their snores.

In the Hebrew, however, the irony works on a literary rather than a purely vernacular plane, making a sharp critique not just of the Jews but of Judaism. The narrative voice is no longer that of a beggar but of an educated Jew at some remove from the scene described. The sense of the words, though, is the same in the Hebrew as in the Yiddish. Here too, the beggars are snoring, but the Hebrew construction, *chotem el chotem koré* (nose calls to nose) echoes Ps. 42: 8, *tehom el tehom koré* (deep calls to deep): the majesty of God's creation is implicitly compared not with the sound of mighty cataracts, as in the psalms, but with this filthy, hungry band of beggars snoring away among the goats and synagogue mice.[9] The grotesque mutations of Jewish life in the Pale are emphasized in further allusions: *vi di poritzim* becomes *kivenei melakhim* (like princes), with its dissonant association of holiness, chosenness, and past glory (Shab. 67a). *A mechaye geven tzu zehn* is transformed into the two words, *ashrei ayin* (happy is the eye), again transporting the reader into a world destroyed but kept alive in the Jewish religious imagination, in which the Temple was the symbol of religious glory and political power. These words appear in the *musaf* (Additional Service) of Yom Kippur, in an elaborate, pathos-ridden description of the Temple service by the medieval Hebrew poet Solomon ibn Gabirol: 'Happy the eye that saw all this, our soul grieves at the mere mention of it.' The synagogue is the survival of the Temple and the beggars are the priests' heirs. 'Happy the eye' is thus twisted from being a statement of past glory to an ironic comment on present misery.

[9] Another satiric case of 'deep calling to deep' occurs in P. G. Wodehouse's *Very Good, Jeeves* (London, 1930) in connection with the digestive disorders and romance of Bertie Wooster's Uncle George and Mrs Wilberforce, though the parallel brings out the sharper and more subtle use in the Hebrew.

A parallel irony appears at the start of *The Beggar Book*, in a scene which recalls, and is possibly influenced by, the comic collision of Dr Slop and Obadiah in *Tristram Shandy*, which Abramowitz had read in Russian translation. Mendele and Alter, both booksellers saying their morning prayers on their wagons, collide in a muddy stream. A band of gentile boys help them out, mocking them in the bargain. All the hapless pair can do, dressed in what Mendele calls their 'priestly' garments—their *tallit* and *tefillin*—is to urge them on, in the Hebrew, *dachafu heitev, heitev dachafu* (lit. push well, well push), again a mocking reference to the Temple service by an allusion to the description in the liturgy of the preparation of the holy incense (*pitum haketoret*) by the high priest, which was accompanied by the exhortation, *hedek heitev, heitev hedek* (grind well, well grind) (Ker. 6*b*). This allusion to a glorious past makes even more unbearable the sense of shame and degradation felt by Jews such as Mendele who retained pride in their past.

The Hebrew satire continues by rendering *mekubolim iz taki oyf der velt gut* (Kabbalists really have it soft in the world) with *akh tov labatlanim ba'olam hazeh* (idlers surely have it good in this world), for *akh tov* immediately calls to mind Psalm 23, with its affirmation of the rewards of faith: 'Surely goodness (*akh tov*) and mercy shall follow me all the days of my life and I shall dwell in the house of the Lord forever.' Is this sleep of exhaustion which Fishke witnesses as an all-too-familiar sight in the Pale a reward of faith, of being chosen? Is this dwelling of paupers in the house of the Lord a privilege? Or a curse? The parodic encomium of beggary reaches its shrill peak with the phrase, unparalleled in the Yiddish, *mi bakabtzanim yidmeh lahem umi yishveh lahem* (who is like unto them among the beggars, who can be compared unto them), again a mocking allusion to the *nishmat* prayer: *mi yidmeh lakh umi yishveh lakh umi ya'arokh lakh* (who is like unto thee, who is equal to thee, who can be compared unto thee), where the subject, again, is not beggars, but God.

4. *IN THE VALLEY OF TEARS*

The Kabtzansker *ba'alei batim* are, Heaven preserve you! great paupers, with not a broken groschen to their name. The only livelihood in Kabtzansk is the beggar-sack, one to the other, from door to door. No sooner does one try to make a living, say, by opening a little shop, than a host of little shops spring up overnight with shopkeepers liberal as manure and not a customer in sight. It's the same with everything: one pushes in on the other, one tramples the other's feet in a wholly Yiddisher style. Where there's two, a third butts in; where there's three, a fourth, and so on and so on, until there's a regular ingathering of exiles, sticking together, all brotherly in strangulating embrace, grabbing one from the other. Such powerful unity of paupery—each creeping into the other's purse, each snatching the God-given crust from the other's mouth—'so long as we're together, neither mine nor yours'—this is one of the fine qualities found uniquely among the Kabtzansker Jews, and for this reason they are privileged to beg from door to door . . .

די קאָבצאַנסקער בעלי־הבּתּים זענען, נישט פאַר אײַך געדאַכט! גרױסע אביונים, האָבּען נישט, איהר זאָלט זאָגען, אַ צוברֿאָכענעם גראָשען בּײַ דער נשמה. אין קאָבצאַנסק אַלײן איז פאַר זײ נישטאָ קײן שום פרנסה, סײדען אײנער צום אַנדערען מיט אַ טאָרבע אין די הײזער אַרומצוגעהן. זאָל פרײוועןַ אײנער מאַכען עפּיס אַ געשעפּטיל, אַ קלײטיל אַ שטײגער, באַלד טאַקי טהוט איהם דער איבעריגער עולם נאָך, און וויעפיל יודען אַזױ פיעל קלײטלעך. קרעמער זענען דאָ װי מיסט און אַ קונה נישט אײנער. דעסגלײַכען איז אין אַנדערע זאַכען. איטליכער האָט ליעבּ אַרײַנצושטופּען זיך אין דער מיט, אָנצוטרעטען יענעם אױף'ן פוס גאַנץ יודישלִיך; װאװ צווײי, זאָל ער זײן אַ דריטער, װאװ דרײַ — אַ פערטער און אַזױ אַלץ ווײַטער, ווײַטער, בּיז עם קומט אױס " קיבּצנו יחד", אַלע קבצנים אינאײעם שטיקלען־זיך־צונױף, חאַפּען זיך אַרום גאָר בּרידערליך און וערעןַ אַזױ דערשטיקטיקט, פערהאַפּט אַלע אױף אײן מאָל. אַזאַ שטאַרקע אַחדות, דאָס הײסט, אַרײַנצוקריכען מיט אַ פוס צו יענעם אין בּײַטעל, אײנער בּײם אַנדערען דעם בּיסען פונ'ם מױל אַרױסצונעמהמען, װאָס גאָט גיט, אַבּי אינאײנעם, מיר נישט, דיר נישט — דאָס איז אײנע פון די מדות טובות, װאָס געפינען זיך נאָר טאַקי בּײַ קאָבצאַנסקער יודען. און אין דעם זכות קומט זײ טאַקי אױס אײנער צום אַנדערען אין די הײזער אַרומצוגעהן . . . ¹⁰

הקבציאלים קבצנים גמורים הם, לא עליכם, והפרוטה אינה מצויה בכיסם. בקבציאל גופא אין שום פרנסה לפניהם אלא זו, שמחזורים על הפתחים זה לזה ומתפרנסים זה מזה ומסיגים זה גבולו של זה. עמד אחד ופתח לו חנות, מיד בני העיר באים ויורדים לפרנסתו, ומספר יהודים הן חנויותיהם. החנונים מרובים והקונים מעטים. וכיוצא בה אתה רואה בשאר העניִנים. כל אחד נכנס לתוך רשות חברו ודוחקו, כהלכת גוברין יהודאין, במקום ששנים עומדים בא השלישי, ובמקום שלשה בא הרביעי, וכך הם מוסיפים ובאים ומצטרפים למנין, לקיים מה שנאמר: "וקבצנו יחד" — כל הקבצנים חבורה אחת, והאי חברותא להם מיתותא... אחדות משונה זו, שכל אחד נטפל לחברו ואומר: יהי חלקי עמך, כלומר, גם לך גם לי לא יהיה — זוהי באמת אחת מהמדות הטובות, שאין אתה מוצאן אלא ביהודים קבציאלים בלבד, ובגלל הדבר הזה זכו לחזר על הפתחים ולגמול חסד זה לזה . . . (145)

In the Valley of Tears is, as its name suggests, the most lachrymose of Mendele's novels: it shows perhaps more than any other work of his the devastating effect of the pogroms on his style and outlook. The Yiddish title *Dos vinshfingerl* (The Magic Ring), kept in each of the three Yiddish versions, refers to science as a panacea for human ills. This might have been appropriate in the age of reform and optimism

---

¹⁰ *Ale verk*, IV. 3–4.

when the 1865 version appeared, but then it was no more than a short story whose chief importance is historical. The retention of the title in the sophisticated post-pogrom versions, when it was clear that no 'magic ring' existed, may be seen either as a sign of the perverse faith of an ageing ideologue who could find no viable alternative to Haskalah, or, more likely, as an ironic comment upon the content of the novel. In so far as the novel maintains ironic distance, which it does in its first quarter, it succeeds as a tragi-comic satire in which the horror of the conditions described is relieved by Mendele's inventiveness and mocking wit. The remainder of the novel, however, dissolves into a rather dull, rambling narrative lacking the sharp irony and charm of Mendele's other works.

The population explosion among the Jews in the Pale—by the end of the nineteenth century there were about five million—created an immense economic burden. The high birth-rate and unemployment are satirized in the opening of *In the Valley of Tears* without giving the full social and political background: here, as elsewhere, there could be no mention of the restrictive laws, culminating in the so-called May Laws of 1882, which limited the movements and the economic opportunities of the Russian Jews. As a result, they often found themselves unemployed or hopelessly in competition not just with other Jews but also with the local gentiles, who bitterly resented them. Simplifications and distortion of theories of Malthus and Darwin, among others, that excess population would inevitably die out or emigrate, or that the strong would survive at the expense of the weak, could all too readily be applied to the Jews of the Pale. The image of the Jews as a species, swarming with aggressive promiscuity like ants or bugs, recurs disturbingly in Mendele's writings, as we shall see in Chapter 3, though never without an element of compassion.

Part of Mendele's irony, as in *The Beggar Book*, lies in making a pretence of seeing these creatures as somehow blessed: cut-throat economic competition and a crab-in-the-sack mentality are identified not as signs of racial prejudice and internal discord but of a unique quality, of 'unity of paupery', an 'ingathering of exiles' (playing on the word *kabetzeinu*, in the liturgical sense of the return to the Land of Israel, and *kabtzan*, a beggar engaged in the ingathering of alms), for which these miserable beggars have reason to feel privileged. It is possible, though unlikely, that Mendele intended the irony here to rebound upon itself, as indeed happened: the poverty which he satirized did lead to a unity of purpose and an 'ingathering of exiles' among those few Russian Jews who turned to Zionism at the time. It was not inappropriate, therefore, that the first issue of *Hashiloach*, the literary journal of the proto-Zionist Hovevei Zion (Lovers of Zion) movement, edited by the Zionist philosopher Ahad Ha'am, opened with *In the Valley of Tears*, which it went on to serialize over the next decade.

As in the passages quoted earlier, the rich allusiveness of the Hebrew brings out not just the irony of a once-great people degraded, but also the possibility of their renewal. Here is a translation of the Hebrew, giving some of the sources and allusions.

The Kabtzielites are total beggars, may this not befall you [Lam. 1: 12], they have not a penny in their purse [S of S Rab. 2: 5]. In Kabtziel itself there is no livelihood but going from door to door [Mish. Ket. 13: 3], living one off the other, encroaching on one another's territory [Deut. 19: 14]. If one opens a shop, the other townsmen straightaway open shops of their own [lit. descend into his livelihood; *Bava metzia* 38*b*]: as many as the number of Jews are their shops [Jer. 2: 28]. The shops are many and the buyers few [Mish. Hag. 1: 5], and the same applies in other respects. Each enters the other's territory, pushing him out in the manner of Jewish men [the *ketubah*—Jewish marriage contract]. When there are two a third comes along [Baraita of R. Ishmael, beg. *Sifra*], when there are three a fourth comes, and so they increase until they make a quorum of ten [Ethics of the Fathers 3: 7], to fulfil the words 'And gather us together' [Amidah prayer, *Teka*]. All the beggars are one band, and this fellowship is death to all [Ta'an. 23*a*] . . . this strange unity in which each latches onto the other, saying, let my portion be with you [Shab. 118*b*], meaning it shall be neither mine nor yours [1 Kgs. 3: 26]—this is truly one of the fine qualities [Deut. Rab. 3: 6] which you find only among the Jews of Kabtziel: for this reason they are so privileged to go from door to door and to give charity one to the other. (145)

Here as elsewhere, the transpositions from the Yiddish—*a tzubro-chener groschen* (a broken groschen) to *vehaperuta einah metzuyah* (they have not a penny); *ganz Yiddishlich* (wholly Yiddisher) to the Aramaic *kehilkhot guvrin yehudain* (in the way of Jewish men); *mir nicht, dir nicht* (neither mine nor yours) to *gam lekha gam li lo yiheyeh* (it shall be neither mine nor yours)—almost invariably move from the vernacular to the literary, though some of the ironic Hebrew usages—*vekabetzenu yachad* (gather us together) and *midot tovot* (fine qualities)—appear in both languages. In addition, there are direct quotes from Deuteronomy and from the story of the judgment of Solomon in 1 Kgs; adaptations of classical constructions, notably the one from Jer. 2: 28, 'as many as your cities are your gods, O Judah'; reversals such as the one from tractate *Ta'anit*, which reads (again in Aramaic), *o chavruta o mituta* (either fellowship or death); and perhaps most ingenious of all, in the description of the ascending number of Jewish businessmen, an ironic echo from Ethics of the Fathers of the descending number of Jewish scholars needed for the *shekhinah* (divine presence) to appear: the businessmen proliferate until they reach a quorum, whereas the scholars begin with a quorum and diminish to one, a bare minimum for the divine presence. The implicit message, in this allusion as in the entire passage, is that the Jews have been degraded from a spiritual people to one obsessed and tormented by the grind of material existence.[11]

5. *OF BYGONE DAYS*

Reb Shloyme deserves credit for tactfully helping me out of my confusion. He reopened the conversation with the guests, and thus broke the ice, so that in a short time they were all talking at once. Everyone knows that authors are naturally gossipy and more talkative than women; the minute they open their mouths they overflow like a river, pouring out nine-tenths of all the words in the world. I too opened my mouth to show that I could talk endlessly with the best of them. They liked me for that, and we became friends instantly, as Jews will.[12]

לאָנג לעבּען זאָל רב שלמה, וואָס ער האָט זיך דערבּאַרימט און רײדענדיג געמאַכט די געסט,
אבּי אַ אָנהויבּ, איז שוין דאָס ווייטערדיגע געגאַנגען וי אַ מזמור, גערעדט הויך אויף אַ קול.
דאָס איז דאָך ידוע, אַז מחברים זענען גרויסע פּלוידערזעק, רײדען מעהר וי וויבּער, וי בּאַלד
עס עפֿענט זיך זײ דאָס מויל, שיטען זיך רײד, וי פֿון אַ לעכערדיגען זאַק. איך האָבּ אויך געעפֿנט
מײן מויל און האָב געוויזען, וואָס איך קען, גערעדט אָהן אויפֿהער. דאָס איז זײ געפֿעלען
געוואָרען, און מיר זענען געוואָרען בּאַלד, וי עס פֿיהרט זיך בּיי יודען, אמת׳ע ידידים... גוטע
בּרידער, הײסט עס.[13]

יתברך רבי שלמה, שנתעורר ברחמים וידובב את המסובים והתחילו כלם כאחד מדברים בקול.
הכל יודעים שהמחברים פטפטנים הם ודברנים יותר מנשים, וכיון שפותחים את פיהם נעשה
כמעין המתגבר ותשעה קבין מלין יוצאים ממנו. אף אני "בפצח פצחתי" והריקותי להם
ניב־שפתים עד בלי די. וזה נתן חני חני בעיניהם ונעשינו מיד, כמנהג היהודים, ידידים אהובים.
(255)

Of Bygone Days is Mendele's last major work, the most directly auto-biographical of his fiction. It also marks the culmination of his move

---

[11] This ironic contrast between the past glory of the Jews and their present day degradation was noted by Coleridge: 'The two images farthest removed from each other which can be comprehended under one term, are, I think, Isaiah—"Hear O heavens, and give ear, O earth!"—and Levi of Holywell Street—"Old clothes!"—both of them Jews, you'll observe.' *Specimens of the Table Talk*, 4th edn. (London, 1851), 271–2.

[12] Tr. R. Sheindlin in Ruth R. Wisse (ed.), *A Shtetl and Other Stories* (New York, 1973), 260.   [13] *Ale verk*, I. ii, p. xiv.

from satire to social realism in the latter part of his career, and is one of the fullest and most beautiful evocations of *shtetl* life. Like most of his other longer works, *Of Bygone Days* had a quirky publishing history which is interesting and revealing in its own right. The Introduction, from which the passage above is taken, was first published in Hebrew in 1894, a Yiddish version of which appeared together with the first book (sixteen chapters) in 1899; and the Hebrew version of the first book and six chapters of Book Two appeared in instalments between 1903 and the end of the First World War: the Yiddish draft of the six chapters was also published during this period. Despite its fitful composition, and although it was apparently left unfinished at the author's death in 1917, *Of Bygone Days* conveys the impression of artistic symmetry and wholeness. The Introduction presents Reb Shloyme, the ageing, successful author, in Odessa holding court with a group of writers on a stormy night. Mendele the Bookpeddler comes in, through the servants' entrance, to meet his creator. The discussion and gossip which follows is interrupted by a knock at the door, and a Lithuanian yeshivah student of about 17 is let in. The boy has no money or shelter and asks to sleep in the school next door. Reb Shloyme, who is also the headmaster of the school, refuses in a flash of anger; the boy is sent back into the storm. This cruel act is triggered off in part by Reb Shloyme's instant perception that the boy is a mirror-image of himself at the same age—a poor, homeless, wandering *Litvak*—and is a symbolic renunciation of this earlier existence. Reb Shloyme is then plagued by his own hypocrisy and, after a sleepless night, he guiltily resolves to tell the story of his early life, a symbolic admission of the young man that he once was. Mendele is conveniently there to go over the manuscript and arrange for its publication.

Significantly, the story does not begin with the author's birth but from age 17—the same age as the young man—after the author's father had died and his mother had remarried; a time of depression and confusion when he began to write, and the Mendelesque spirit of mockery first stirred in him.[14] The second chapter goes further back in time, to the author's childhood, when his family was intact. From then on, the narrative is chronological, following the growth of the author and of his artistic vocation until his father's death and his own consequent wanderings in the Pale, when he lived the hard life of an

---

[14] 'Autobiographical Notes', 3; see also ch. 5.

indigent yeshivah student. This narrative has a cyclical effect as it reaches approximately the age of 17 and so links up with the first chapter and the Introduction.

Mendele's arrival at Reb Shloyme's creates a conversational bottle-neck among the writers, who turn their noses up at this tramp-like figure bringing dirt into the house. Reb Shloyme, however, has a warm regard for Mendele (though his familiarity shows traces of contempt) as a wit and a devotee of books, and also as one who values his own art and can facilitate its publication. He eases Mendele into the group, and they quickly accept him. In describing this scene, however, Mendele has his revenge for their initial coldness; he emerges as a worthy alter-ego to Reb Shloyme. The Hebrew alludes to the prayerbook's exalted picture of the ministering angels who 'open their mouths' (*potechim et pihem*) in holiness and purity and with pure speech and holy melody 'respond in unison' (*kulam ke'echad onim*) in praise of the Lord (Morning Service, *hame'ir la'aretz*). The association of angelic purity of speech with this rather petty, self-important lot is then deflated with references to women's talk: women may be chatterboxes, according to the Talmud (Ber. 48*b*), but writers are worse; of ten measures of speech which God granted the world (Kid. 49*b*), the writers took nine. As there is nothing creative or admirable in this chatter, the use of the simile *kema'ayan hamitgaber* (like a stream flowing with ever-sustained vigour) is an ironic slap at them: it is borrowed from Rabbi Yochanan ben Zakkai's description of his imaginative pupil Eleazar ben Arach (Ethics of the Fathers 2: 8).

Mendele responds with animation, which he describes as his shell cracking open (*befetzach patzachti*)—again an allusion to the angels, this time in Simeon ben Abun's medieval *piyut*, *Kol shinaneh shachak*, recited on Rosh Hashana, and he joins in the chatter, 'pouring down upon them of the overwhelming fruit of the lips', a distortion of Mal. 3: 10, 'And I will pour down for you an overwhelming blessing'—'fruit of the lips' (*niv-sefatayim*) is borrowed from Isa. 57: 19 and inserted instead of 'blessing' (*berakhah*). A satiric *coup de grâce* is then administered with a reference to the Exodus: 'and the Lord had given the people favour in the sight of the Egyptians, so that they let them have what they asked' (Exod. 12: 36). The picture of enmity dissipated, exaggeratedly, into instant friendship turns on itself, for in the act of describing this 'friendship', Mendele effectively brings an eleventh plague upon the writers, that of satire.

The falsity of this familiarity is contrasted with the deep and genuine though ambivalent bond between Reb Shloyme, Mendele, and the boy who appears strategically a few moments later, at the climax of a heated argument about the nature of art. Theory gives way to practice as the author gives an obvious clue to his own creative motivation, to the explosive mixture of realism, caricature, and bias in his art. In the momentary intersection of the three figures, the author in effect presents three projections of himself: Reb Shloyme, the author more or less as he was; Mendele, the embodiment in caricature of suppressed aspects of Reb Shloyme; the boy, the rejected self-image of the artist as a young man. This split between author and character is a vital ingredient in Mendele's art and is the subject of Chapter 2.

Mendele's reworking of the five novels from Yiddish into Hebrew contributed directly to the emergence of modern Hebrew literary style and indirectly to the growth of vernacular Hebrew. (Ironically, Yiddish, the vernacular of Mendele's age, is now mainly the province of scholarship, while much that was once purely literary in Hebrew has become part of modern usage.) This body of work is the chief cultural marking of the transition from a medieval, Germanic, orthodox Jewish sensibility to a secular, modern Semitic one, fully conscious of the ancient Hebraic associations of national independence, power, and achievement. In his mastery and satiric manipulation of the classical sources, Mendele did for Hebrew what Joyce did for Greek myth in *Ulysses*: he adapted the ancient world-view to a modern sensibility, denying through mock-heroic satire the sacred authority of the sources but implicitly accepting their imperishable value and their power to inspire. He did more than that: in viciously portraying the degradation of the broken mare, he unexpectedly turned it back into a prince.

2

Mendele and Abramowitz: Anatomy of Self-Caricature

MENDELE THE BOOKPEDDLER, like Chaplin's Tramp, is not identical with his creator,[1] but many details in the portrait of Mendele are transparently based upon Abramowitz's own experiences and psychology. Mendele is in some ways a caricature of the author, revealing more truth in its distortion than a photograph in true likeness. Like the Tramp, Mendele's existence derives mainly from the author's memories of the past, particularly his adolescence after his father's death, when he lived as a wandering down-and-out: in fact, most of Abramowitz's novels are set during the reign of Nicholas I, when he was growing up, though the Hebrew versions were all written during the reign of Nicholas II, over forty years later. During this latter period, Abramowitz (like Chaplin from his mid-20s onwards) was comfortably established, well fed, impeccably dressed and groomed, and enjoyed immense acclaim. It is initially puzzling that for all his good fortune he remained to the end of his life obsessed with half-starved, comically bedraggled beggars. In the 1888 Yiddish dedication of *Fishke the Lame* (*The Beggar Book*), he confesses:

It has been my lot to descend to the depths, to the cellars of Jewish life. My stock in trade is: rags and mouldy wares. My dealings are with paupers and beggars, the poor wretches of life; with degenerates, cripples, charlatans and other unfortunates, the dregs of humanity. I always dream of beggars. Before my eyes, I always see a basket soaring—the old familiar Jewish beggar basket.[2]

[1] See e.g. Nachman Mayzel (ed.), *Dos Mendele buch* (The Mendele Book), (New York, 1959), 294–325; and Miron, *A Traveler Disguised*, 130–68. On the contradictions involved in Mendele's role as storyteller, character, and 'rhetorical figure', see Shalom Luria, 'Halashon hafigurativit bitzirato haduleshonit shel Mendele Mocher Sefarim, (Figurative language in the bilingual works of Mendele Mocher Sefarim), Ph.D dissertation, The Hebrew University, Jerusalem, 1977. For a discussion of Mendele as 'a collection of incoherent identities' whose narrative multiplicity is a form of liberation from the pressures of Jewish life under tsarist rule, see Jeffrey Fleck, 'Mendele in Pieces', *Prooftexts* 3/2 (1983), 169–88.

[2] Tr. Stillman, *Fishke the Lame*, 15.

The similarities between Abramowitz and Chaplin go deeper: in-fluenced by Dickens (whom Abramowitz read in Russian translation), both confront childhood loss and family disruption, squalid poverty, anxiety and madness, with a bittersweet mixture of laughter and senti-ment, pathos and tears. Both had the rare gift of being able to move rapidly from comedy to tragedy and back, and both were strongly aware of the tragic premiss underlying their comedy. Abramowitz's comic yet heart-rending portraits of maltreated animals, notably *The Mare* and 'The Calf', recall Chaplin's account of a childhood memory as an anticipation of his films. In their concern for animals, these stories were directly autobiographical: a close acquaintance recalled that the author 'was deeply sensitive to all suffering creatures and did not discriminate between men and animals; men were like animals to him, and he regarded animals as if they possessed human souls'.[3] This sensitivity is vivid in 'The Calf', in which the intensity of a boy's attachment to a calf (like Israel's to the mare in *The Mare*) is clearly an offshoot of his father's death: the calf is an 'orphan', like him (356). His mother, unable to provide for him, sends him to a yeshivah—this was Abramowitz's own experience after his father died. Meanwhile, the calf matures and gives birth to a calf of her own. The calf has to be slaughtered and the boy has this nightmare:

I saw a tender eight-day calf running from the slaughterer, hiding its head under a man's coat, bleating in tears. The man pushed it away, saying, 'Go, you were created for the slaughter!' The poor calf was tied, screaming for its mother—Meh-meh! The mother was in the field. She could not hear its last cry to her before death. The butcher held it down to the ground, stuck his foot on it, held its neck—the slaughterer, the plucking of the hairs, the uncovering of the neck, the knife, 'Blessed be Thou . . .' and the blood, the gurgling, the shudder, the death-groan! (361)

A parallel incident is related by Chaplin in his autobiography. Like the boy in 'The Calf', he had no inkling of the animal's fate. As in Abramowitz's case, the horrified realization that it would be slaughtered might be interpreted as a 'screen memory', both disguising and be-traying a whole aspect of childhood, particularly the effects of family break-up.

At the end of our street was a slaughterhouse, and sheep would pass our house on the way to be butchered. I remember one escaped and ran down the street,

[3] Rav Tzair, *Masekhet zikhronot*, 31.

to the amusement of onlookers. Some tried to grab it and others tripped over themselves. I had giggled with delight at its lambent capering and panic, it seemed so comic. But when it was caught and carried back into the slaughter-house, the reality of the tragedy came over me and I ran indoors, screaming and weeping to Mother, 'They're going to kill it! They're going to kill it!'[4]

These glimpses of the lower depths of existence later found a creative outlet, in the Tramp and in Mendele, through which the horror could be mastered in comedy.

Much of the comic satire in Abramowitz and Chaplin is based on the premiss of fallen aristocracy and the denial, against all evidence to the contrary, of poverty and degradation. Both had known a comfort-able, even comparatively aristocratic, life prior to the break-up of their families, and the characters of Mendele and the Tramp preserve discordant traces of this ur-existence: Mendele, his rabbinic erudition, his taste in books, and sensitivity; and the Tramp, his suit, hat, and cane, as well as his genteel manners, all of which clash with his en-vironment of grimy alleys and doss-houses. There are, in addition, strong undercurrents of subversion in both characters: Mendele's learning, an emblem of Jewish aristocracy, is used not for a religious ideal but often to mock the ideal in relation to the miseries of the present; the Tramp, well bred as he apparently is, is not above taking candy from a baby, or kicking a lady in the rear, as occasion requires. Both the satiric comedy and the social criticism are spiced with a generous dose of anti-authoritarianism, Mendele's toward communal leaders and religious authorities, and the Tramp's toward the upper class and the police.

Abramowitz also shared with Chaplin an extraordinary ability to identify with his characters, an almost ectoplasmic gift for getting under their skins and becoming them: for this reason, it is not surpris-ing that both are so closely identified with their principal creations. Abramowitz's secretary, David Eynhorn, left an intriguing account of his writing technique, which brings to mind the 'method' school of acting.

He was not dictating; he impersonated, acted like a performer on the stage. In front of my eyes living characters began to hover. They gesticulated, talked, and eventually evaporated . . . And so he would stand without a rest for four

---

[4] Charles Chaplin, *My Autobiography* (New York, 1966), 31. On screen memories, see David Aberbach, 'Screen Memories of Writers', *International Review of Psycho-Analysis*, 10/1 (1983), 47–62. An example of a screen memory in Mendele is quoted on p. 95 below.

hours, sob, laugh, get angry, quarrel, talk like a merchant, like an old Jewish woman, like a *rov*, like a *maskil*, mimicking each in his turn.[5]

Similar recollections of the artist's uncommon identification with his creations are found among those who worked for Chaplin. Robert Parrish, for instance, recalled the rehearsal for the scene in *City Lights* in which the Tramp is helping the blind girl across the street, and he played one of the news-boys with pea-shooters.

He showed us how he would walk, how he would twirl his cane, how he would tip his hat, how he would smile at Virginia Cherrill and so on. Then he became Virginia Cherill, the beautiful blind girl, and the tramp at the same time, jumping from one position to the other, twirling his cane, holding his hands out in front of his 'sightless' eyes.

As he passed in front of our corner, Austin Jewell and I raised our pea-shooters. Chaplin said, 'No, wait!' and promptly stopped being the tramp and the blind girl and became two news-boys blowing pea-shooters. He would blow a pea and then run over and pretend to be hit by it, then go back to blow another pea. He became a kind of dervish, playing all the parts, using all the props, seeing and cane-twirling as the tramp, not seeing and grateful as the blind girl, pea-shooting as the news-boys. Finally he had it all worked out and reluctantly gave us back our parts. I felt that he would much rather have played all of them himself.[6]

In some ways, the character of Mendele changed greatly in the fifty-odd years of his creation. The rather crass, even cruel Mendele of the 1864–5 draft of *The Parasite* is quite unlike the mature Mendele of the later stories—the same is true of the Tramp in the early and late films. In fact, in each story the use of Mendele varies to suit Abramowitz's purposes. The buffoonish foil to the tailor in 'Shem and Japheth in the Train' would not necessarily be identified with the highly complex tragi-comic figure in 'Warsaw 1881'. Similarly, the characterization of Mendele in the introductions to *The Mare, The Travels of Benjamin the Third, In the Valley of Tears*, and *Of Bygone Days* is sketchy, to say the least, alongside of the wonderfully human if somewhat caricaturistic portrayal of Mendele in *The Beggar Book*.

Yet, although Mendele's character became richer and more complex in the course of a half-century, the main outline of his personality remained constant. That he was not meant to be identified with Abramowitz is clear in the Introduction to *Of Bygone Days*, where, for

---

[5] Quoted by Miron, *A Traveler Disguised*, 80–1.
[6] Robert Parrish, *Growing Up in Hollywood* (London, 1976), 43.

the first and only time, author and character come face to face. Mendele is an orthodox Jew with skullcap, earlocks, and *tzitzit*; Abramowitz was a largely assimilated Jew. Mendele is somewhat naïve, unworldly, and ignorant; Abramowitz was highly educated for his time. Mendele is nearly always away from his hometown, Kesalon—at one point, we learn, he has not seen his wife and family for two years; Abramowitz was very much a patriarchal figure, surrounded by family. Mendele sells books; Abramowitz writes them. Like the naïve persona in Chaucer's *Troilus and Criseyde*, with his ironic references to 'myn aucteur', Mendele is consistently depicted as merely telling a story. He is not a true writer, he writes in the Introduction to *The Travels of Benjamin the Third*, and his efforts, such as they are, are inferior. He is usually given a text or told a story which he then 'improves' or 'translates' and prepares for publication. Like Chaucer's narrator, he professes to have no real artistic instinct (though his introductions are works of art), but is content to act as a medium for other, superior talents.

Mendele belongs to a world which Abramowitz left behind. His poverty, provincialism, lack of self-esteem, religious observance and appearance, superstition, and naïvety were once Abramowitz's, but no longer. In so far as these disabilities still afflicted the author, he apparently tried to escape or overcome them.

Mendele is generally hard-up: in the Yiddish Introduction to *The Mare*, he bewails the fact that his horse died of starvation because he could not afford to feed it. In 'The Exchange', he tells his wife that if she needs money while he is away she should pawn her jewellery and household things (457). He describes the shocking state of his house and clothes: 'the ceiling sags, the roof is broken, a wall slants, panes are missing in the windows . . . my shoe has split open and let dust and filth in . . . and my *kapote*, too, hints that its days of service are over, for it's nothing but a thing of shreds and patches' ('Shelter from the Storm', 383). Abramowitz had known such poverty, but mainly in adolescence after his father's death, although in one later time of hardship, in the late 1860s, he was forced into Mendele's profession and became an itinerant bookseller selling his own books.[7] Clearly, for most of his adult life he was far removed from the constant, shabby, anxious destitution of Mendele. In fact, during the second half of his life, as headmaster of the school in Odessa, he had a degree of

---

[7] Klausner, *Historia shel hasifrut ha'ivrit hachadashah*, vi. 350.

security, success, and veneration rare among Jewish writers of the time. In contrast with the unkempt, muddy Mendele, he was fastidious in dress and led a clean, bourgeois, well-ordered life in one place. Contrary to the image of decrepitude called up by Mendele, Abramowitz even in old age had a fine physique. He loved swimming in the Black Sea and walking long distances in the countryside near Odessa. The writer Jacob Fichman, who knew him well in his last years, remembered how 'he moved among us like a king with his upright bearing'.[8]

Mendele, in contrast, suffers from low self-esteem; the reader will recall that when he visited Reb Shloyme, he entered via the servants' entrance, through the kitchen (*Of Bygone Days*, 254). Similarly, in 'Earthquake Days', after Mendele and his companion Reb Leib arrive in the town of Shichor ('Blackville', based on Odessa, on the Black Sea) during the pogroms, 'we exhausted ourselves finding a place suitable for us and appropriate to our worth—a narrow, dark garret' (406).

Mendele, however, is the image of what Abramowitz once was, and to an extent remained, psychologically. He was rooted to the past, to Mendele's world, to the haunting memories and anxieties which robbed him of sleep or gave him nightmares of beggars.[9] At that time, when he lived among beggars or frequently came into contact with them, he might have entered homes of the wealthy through the servants' entrance.

In religious observance, too, Mendele resembles the young Abramowitz, not the mature artist. He keeps the fast of 17 Tammuz, the anniversary of the breach of the walls of Jerusalem by Nebuchadrezzar in 587 BCE; Abramowitz, in contrast, was so unobservant that his wife, who was apparently more religious, or more concerned with appearances, than he, reportedly had to force him to go to synagogue on the High Holy Days.[10] Mendele normally puts on *tallit* and *tefillin* and prays (*The Beggar Book*, 91); Abramowitz did not, though at the end of his life he returned to the orthodoxy of his youth.[11] Mendele would

---

[8] Jacob Fichman, 'Be'or hashekiyah' (Mendele's Twilight Years), in *Kol kitvei Mendele Mocher Sefarim* (Collected Works of Mendele Mocher Sefarim), 1922 edn., IV, vii. 222.

[9] On Mendele's insomnia, which he connected with traumatic childhood memories, see Fichman, ibid. On his constant nightmares of beggars see the dedication of *Fishke the Lame*, quoted on p. 28 above.

[10] See Klausner, *Historia shel hasifrut ha'ivrit hachadashah*, vi. 391.

[11] Chaim Nachman Bialik, 'U-Mendele zaken' (Mendele in Old Age), in *Kol kitvei Chaim Nachman Bialik* (Collected Works of Chaim Nachman Bialik), (Tel Aviv, 1958), 251.

not dream of profaning the Sabbath, whereas Abramowitz was less than fastidious in his Sabbath observance; according to one account,[12] his wife would snatch the pen from his hand to stop him from writing on the day of rest.

In appearance, too, Mendele is a relic of what Abramowitz once was. Whereas Mendele wears a *kapote* and his head is covered and adorned with sidelocks, Abramowitz did not wear a *kapote*, was not particular about covering his head, and had shaved off his sidelocks as a young man. His sensitive, semi-comic account of the entrance of Mendele and Reb Leib into the grand house of an assimilated Zionist leader (based on Leon Pinsker) in 'Earthquake Days' betrays Abramowitz's own one-time gaucherie in the company of the wealthy and the educated, but this social unease probably did not survive his early manhood.

Lord alone knows how hard it was for us to remove our hats from our heads, which had been covered all the time—nights included—since birth. But the beadle standing by the door did not allow us to wear our hats and even prohibited us from wearing skullcaps. At that moment we felt naked as if in the bathhouse. (410)

His slightly mocking empathy with Mendele's religious customs, despite his own rebellion against traditional observance, is evident also in his portrayal of Mendele's sorrow and indignation after an antisemitic Russian official shaves off his sidelock.

I saw my sidelock lying on the ground and I began to cry. My sidelock! Sidelock of my old age! It had grown with me since childhood and seen much joy and sorrow. My mother would comb and curl it when I was a child—she never had enough of my lovely black curls—and she took great care not to cause a single hair to fall out, God forbid. (*The Beggar Book*, 104)

Mendele's superstitiousness was also shared by Abramowitz up to a point in life. Mendele is depicted in the Introduction to *The Parasite* as a seller not only of books but also of such items as wolves' teeth and amulets. He caters to the superstitions of his clientele and is himself superstitious. In *The Beggar Book*, for instance, he accepts the belief, then commonly held, that the marriage of paupers in a graveyard had power to dispel the plague (97). Similarly, he allows himself to be bled by leeches (98), a medical practice which prevailed at the time.

---

[12] Yitzhak Dov Berkowitz, *Harishonim kivenei adam* (Essays), vol. vii of *Kitvei Y. D. Berkowitz* (Collected Works), (Tel Aviv, 1953), 105.

As a child, Abramowitz had believed in all sorts of similar things, in demons and the Evil Eye, in exorcists and faith-healers, in the transmigration of souls. In *Of Bygone Days*, he tells of these with great charm, and admits, to his own amusement, that like many Jewish children he was raised to believe in the literal truth of biblical and talmudic stories, legends, and superstitions. A lodger in the present, he had his true home in a past fantasy world inhabited by such figures as Abraham, Moses, and Solomon; and for this reason, he adds, 'it's not at all surprising in this crazy, dream-like existence that superstition was rife. Demons, animals in human form and other wild, fantastic creatures had plenty of scope, as it were, in the muddled, unsettled minds of those who believed them to be real' (272).[13] The child's chief defences against the evil spirits who populated this existence were Mendele's own paraphernalia of religious faith and prayer: *tzitzit*, *mezuzah*, and the Shema, 'a tried and tested remedy against the demons' (*The Mare*, 333).

Only much later in life did Abramowitz free himself of such beliefs, using them instead as satiric material in his stories. From his early 20s he was a devotee of rationalism, a nihilist in the sense defined by Bazarov in Turgenev's novel *Fathers and Sons* (a title borrowed by Abramowitz for his first Hebrew novel): one who does not accept any belief or authority on trust, who regards everything from a critical standpoint. While retaining a fascination with psychopathology, throughout the vagaries of his career he remained committed to rationalism and to secular education. It is tempting to link the fact that two of his four daughters became doctors—a remarkable achievement, and certainly for Russian Jewish women, at the time—with his ideology, and specifically his educational writings on medicine.

Mendele, in contrast, is ignorant and naïve in secular matters, though his profession makes him more tolerant of educated Jews such as Reb Shloyme than he might otherwise be, and some of his books for sale are modern. Perhaps the most blatant display of Mendele's ignorance appears in 'Shem and Japheth in the Train'. Sitting in a third-class train carriage with a Jewish tailor and his family who have been expelled as foreigners from Prussia, Mendele overhears the tailor telling his hungry child in a flash of bitter humour that he must wait as 'Bismarck has prohibited food'. The prohibition of food was a

[13] Further discussion of superstition among the Russian Jews is found in ch. 4.

common enough prescription for the sick, but the boy is healthy and this puzzles Mendele.

'Who is this Bismarck who prohibited your healthy son from eating?' I asked.
'Have you never heard of Bismarck? My goodness!'
'What if I don't know him? He must be a doctor, and where I live, in Kesalon, there are hundreds of expert bleeders like him.' (400)

This ignorance is not feigned: when a bedraggled creature emerges from hiding under the seats and behaves as if he belongs to the tailor's family—his identity is revealed later—Mendele admits that 'many explanations and conjectures come to mind to explain this matter and the most likely seemed to be this: apparently this was the Bismarck that my neighbour had spoken of previously' (ibid.). Mendele's ignorance is a comic device bringing light to a scene otherwise black with wretchedness, but is no less genuine for that.

As a young man, Abramowitz had been as glaringly ignorant as Mendele. The Hebrew educator and writer Abraham Ber Gottlober, with whom Abramowitz studied in secret in Kamenets-Podolsk in the early 1850s, recalled his almost total ignorance in secular matters.[14] This was hardly surprising. He had no books, and moreover there was no Hebrew or Yiddish press in Russia at the time. (The first Russian Jewish paper, *Hamelitz*, appeared in 1860, and the first Yiddish paper, *Kol mevaser*, began in 1862 as a supplement to *Hamelitz*.) It is probable that Mendele's ignorance of Bismarck had its parallel in some equally ludicrous gap in Abramowitz's early education, for example who Metternich or Palmerston was. At any rate, he had to undergo a rigorous programme of self-education over a period of several years in order to catch up.

It is probable that Mendele's naïvety is not unlike that of the young Abramowitz. When the tailor in 'Shem and Japheth in the Train' tells Mendele that he and his family are no longer Jewish, and Mendele, uncomprehending, asks why, the tailor replies, 'You don't know the times we're living in' (401)—whereupon Mendele helpfully pulls out a calendar, informs the tailor of the Torah reading that week and, seeing a business opportunity, offers it for sale! As a child, Abramowitz recalls with amused irony, he could hardly imagine a Jew not behaving exactly like the local Jews of Kopyl. When he first heard of a new species of Jew—the *maskil*—he was horrified. 'A Jew—without a hat! A Jew—

[14] Abraham Ber Gottlober, *Zikhronot umasa'ot* (Memories and Journeys), ed. R. Goldberg, vol. ii (Jerusalem, 1976), 14.

eating without washing his hands and saying the blessing? Have the Berlin Jews gone out of their minds? Don't they know what's waiting for them in hell? Traps, fire and brimstone and trails of flame' (277).[15]

In later life, however, he knew too well what assimilation and conversion entailed: as we have seen, his only son, Michael (Meir), converted to Christianity.[16] He did so not out of conviction but to marry a Christian girl whom he loved and could not otherwise marry—Russian law prohibited Jewish men from marrying Christians. He had met her as a student in St Petersburg in the late 1870s. In this time of political ferment, he became active in revolutionary circles. Arrested, he was sent to Siberia for five years. This was a source of the deepest anxiety to his family, especially against the background of violent antisemitism in the early 1880s. The girl, daughter of a wealthy banker, waited for him, and after his release in 1885 he married her. There were two children, but the marriage ended in divorce; after the Bolshevik revolution, Michael returned to Judaism. All this created a scandal among the Jews in the Pale, not only because of the taboo on conversion and intermarriage but also because of Abramowitz's position as a leading Jewish educator and writer. Much as he grieved for his son, he did not sit *shiva* or say *kaddish* for him, as one can imagine Mendele doing if his son had converted. He kept in close touch with him, to the detriment of his reputation: in fact, largely for this reason and amid much controversy, he was denied election as an honorary member of the Odessa Hebrew Literary Society. The story 'Shem and Japheth in the Train' might be read as a gentle justification for conversion: everyone would be 'Jewish' if driven to it as the gentile is and, by the same token, conversion to Christianity is neither more nor less than a strategy for survival.

Abramowitz's relationship with his son is a touchstone of the differences between the author and Mendele and of his ambivalence towards Jews and Judaism. Michael Abramowitz's upbringing was almost totally devoid of Jewish education.[17] Mendele's wagon, with its Hebrew books and religious articles, did not reach him. In truth, this must have involved some effort on his father's part as the environment

---

[15] On the Haskalah and the *maskilim* see ch. 4.

[16] On Michael Abramowitz and his conversion to Christianity see Isaac Ramba, 'Madu'a hitnatzer beno shel Mendele?' (Why Did Mendele's Son Convert to Christianity?), *Hado'ar*, 28 June/2 Tammuz, 48/32 (1968), 589–90.

[17] See Joshua Hana Ravnitzky, *Dor vesoferav: Reshimot vedivrei zikhronot al sofrei dori* (Writers I Have Known), vol. ii (Tel Aviv, 1937), 38.

of his early years in Berdichev and Zhitomir was totally Jewish. Most extraordinarily puzzling, even to Abramowitz's greatest admirers, was his attitude to his son after the conversion. He seems to have been in awe of his son, as if he had achieved superiority over ordinary Jews. The Yiddish writer Ephraim Kaganovsky caught a glimpse of this twisted side of Abramowitz on a visit to Abramowitz's home in Odessa with Bialik. Abramowitz turned them both away and Bialik, disgruntled, explained that Michael was visiting. Bialik's allegation that Abramowitz believed his satires to be realistic portraits of the Jews is a damning indictment by Abramowitz's most loyal disciple, the major figure in Hebrew literature among the younger generation.

The old man is embarrassed of his own people in front of his converted son . . . and, even more, of his Christian daughter-in-law . . . He's convinced that all Jews are the way he describes them in his stories. He admires the Patriarchs— Abraham, Isaac, and Jacob. He thinks highly of Moses. But the Jews of his generation are beggars, in his view. [He] doesn't regard his son with the apprehension of an ordinary Jew [towards a convert] . . . He sees in him a superiority because of his civil rights which other Jews do not have . . . That he is allowed to live in Moscow . . . That his wife is not Jewish, but Russian . . . And so, when his son comes to visit, it's a special day . . . not for Jews . . . not for one of us.[18]

Mendele might thus be described as the familiar, embarrassing, lovable image of the traditional, impoverished Jew whom Abramowitz would not have allowed into the house when his son was there. He is, in some ways, an animated fossil of what Abramowitz once was or might have been and remains hauntingly imprinted upon his personality. Upon his fictional character, however, Abramowitz projected many aspects of himself.

Mendele, like Abramowitz, is an orphan bereaved of his father. The sight of the dying father is recalled in *Of Bygone Days*.

Reb Chaim lay delirious, eyes closed, mouth half-open, lips parched. A groan sawed through him. He was barely breathing. His face twisted up at times and he sighed bitterly. Sarah [his wife] leaned over him and spoke to him but he didn't answer. She sat, head bowed, weeping quietly. (292)

A parallel description of the dying father—the repetition suggests how powerful was Abramowitz's memory of it—appears in a nightmare of Mendele's in 'Warsaw 1881'.[19] In hiding during the pogrom, Mendele

---

[18] Ramba, 'Madu'a hitnatzer beno shel Mendele?' 590.
[19] This nightmare is quoted in full in the Conclusion.

has a nightmare in which he returns to childhood to seek refuge at home and finds his father on his death-bed.

> Screaming in terror, I ran to the safety of father's house. I found him, a heap of bones, on a straw mat, covered with a rag. Oy! This—my shelter, rock of my strength, my father in whom I trust! This broken reed—supports a whole family! He provides us with clothes and food! His face is shrunken, his jaw sags, his eyes are dull. His chest rises and falls, shudders and dies away, his breathing grates in his throat.
>
> I mourn, I ache, I'm turned inside out. (426)

Similarly, the autobiographical account of Shloyme's horrified discovery after his father's death that his prestigious seat in synagogue has been sold is matched in Mendele's own experience: both perceive themselves as fallen aristocrats. Reb Chaim's death led to a steep fall in status, painfully brought home to the young Abramowitz in this incident.

> No sooner did Shloyme sit with the important men by the east wall than a man came—the stuffed oaf!—and drove him away. 'Get going, this seat is mine. I paid your mother good money for it.' Shloyme was thunderstruck. In his confusion and distress, the hard words sank in: a boorish stranger now had his father's seat. His sons circled Shloyme's podium, shoving him in the ribs and shoulders. Having no room to move, he turned in embarrassment and found angry, incredulous eyes everywhere: what is *this* doing among us? Like a lost lamb he moved from place to place until he reached the area behind the pulpit near the door, where the poor stand. (*Of Bygone Days*, 296)

Exactly the same incident occurs to the young Mendele in 'Warsaw 1881', though again Mendele's fictional first-person account is more emotionally wrenching than Abramowitz's autobiographical memory in the third person. It is as though the mask of Mendele enables Abramowitz to reveal more than when he speaks directly. The pogroms are the background to this memory, which is set off by the insistence of one of the Jews in hiding that the Jewish people are barred from returning to the Land of Israel until the Messiah comes. Mendele implicitly compares the futility of his attempt to regain his father's seat with the alleged futility of Jewish efforts to re-establish themselves in Palestine. Interestingly, Mendele is an 'only son' (an echo of the story of the binding of Isaac?) whereas Abramowitz had several brothers;[20] and he does not mention, as Shloyme does, that his mother has sold the seat.

---

[20] Cf. Weinreich, 'Mendeles eltern un mitkinder', 270–86.

I was a boy when my father died. Though respected in the community, he left nothing but his prestigious seat by the east wall in the house of study, where he had prayed and studied. I, his only son, well-loved, had stood beside him, basking in the glory, showing off to my friends. Poverty drove me from the home of my widowed, grieving mother. I lived the life of a wandering yeshivah boy, an abandoned, hungry orphan, and I saw much trouble and evil. Meanwhile, the seat was sold. Like a lost lamb, I came home long afterwards, and I went to the house of study which I had missed badly on my travels. Everyone else sat in dignity but for me there was no room. I took courage and went to the old seat by the east wall. My heart was full of love and yearning for it. What a shock I had! A stranger sat on my father's seat. He was the son of a servant-girl whom fortune's wheel had lifted from the dung-heap. Flanked by three sons, fat as calves, he stared at me, surprised, controlling his anger. The sons began to shove me in the ribs and shoulders. Humble, trembling, I made myself small so as not to be in their way, God forbid. Signalling with his finger, he said angrily, 'Go away, you don't belong here!' His sons pushed me harder. I left in tears. (432–3)

The indigent wanderings which followed this humiliation gave Abramowitz first-hand knowledge of the lifestyle and psychology of the beggars and outcasts of the Pale, and in this respect, too, he was at one with Mendele. Later, while living in Berdichev, he helped found a society for poor-relief which brought him into frequent contact with beggars: 'He visited their hiding places, he talked with them a great deal, he took great interest in their way of life—sometimes he would even act as a judge in their petty quarrels.'[21] In his 'Autobiographical Notes', Abramowitz describes his wanderings as pre-ordained in heaven, in common with the prophet Jeremiah (1: 5)—a necessary trial and education, preparing him for his life as a writer and for his archetypal persona as a 'Jew of Jews': Mendele Mocher Sefarim.

It seems that heaven decreed before my birth that I would be a writer for my people, a poor, wretched people, and that the Lord wished that I should learn their ways and study their deeds, so He said to my soul: 'Wander like a bird through my world: poor of the poor, Jew of Jews, will you be on earth.' And the wind bore me, tossed me through life, pushed by the angel of God. It brought me to the lower depths, to my desperately poor brethren, and I lived their sufferings and felt their pain, and I had a double portion of their grief. (3)

In other details, too, Mendele is comparable with Abramowitz: Mendele also has one son and many daughters (Introduction to *The Parasite*; *The Beggar Book*, 105; 'Shelter from the Storm', 383). Many of

---

[21] Klausner, *Historia shel hasifrut ha'ivrit hachadashah*, vi. 344.

his characteristics and views are similar to, if not identical with, those of Abramowitz. Like Abramowitz, he is well acquainted with Scripture and can quote it for his purposes. He is an advocate of Haskalah, though in the crisis caused by the pogroms he concedes the value of the Jewish pioneers in Palestine ('Warsaw 1881', 435). He has a hearty dislike of spoken Hebrew as being contrived and artifical, and in the only passage in Abramowitz's entire *œuvre* in which a character speaks Hebrew, Mendele tells him with comic disgust to speak like a normal human being, in Yiddish ('Earthquake Days', 417). This scene is of considerable historical interest, reminding us that in contrast with the present day, when there are several million Hebrew speakers and the language has achieved impressive versatility, a century ago the language was relatively undeveloped and few could speak it. Abramowitz could not bear to hear Hebrew spoken—to his ear, spoken Hebrew was still too rough and unaesthetic; women speaking Hebrew were his particular bugbear.[22] Finally, Mendele's aim, 'to help our Jewish brethren to the best of my poor ability' (*The Travels of Benjamin the Third*, 57), and his reputation for understanding the spirit and behaviour of the Jewish people ('Earthquake Days', 416), are Abramowitz's.

Various traits which friends and acquaintances noted (usually in a tone of affection rather than criticism) in Abramowitz—his occasional pretentiousness, his capacity for self-deceit, his stinginess, stubbornness, and quick temper, his intolerance of criticism and attitude of superiority—are at least partly evident in the portrayal of Mendele.

Both Mendele and Abramowitz describe the Jews with the superior eye of a natural scientist. Here is Mendele's satiric picture of the ant-like Jews of Kesalon in 'Shelter from the Storm'.

In these ant-men I saw God's miracles—human feelings and incredibly sharp senses to aid survival. The typical Kesalonite ant has two antennae, in the shape of human hands, which he uses to feel everything that comes his way. It has a marvellous organ of smell to sniff out all that is worthwhile, even if it's hidden ten feet underground or stashed in your secret pocket. The little creatures are no Samsons, but they get what they need through clever calculation. Their behaviour with a newcomer: they get all excited and, gathering round, they smell him up, finding out all they can about him with their antennae, doing a crazy sort of dance. For the sake of a piece of bread they band together, seventy-seven of them fighting over the tiniest bit. It always amused me to observe them close up. When I got sick of them—I was sometimes overwhelmed with depression—I would wave my cane or squirt ink at them. Off

[22] See *Igerot Ahad Ha'am* (Letters), ed. A. Simon, vol. vi (Tel Aviv, 1960), 97.

they ran to hide, watching me, rubbing their eyes. Some tried to sneak up and bite, but it hurt as much as a flea. Soon after, they got hungry. They crawled out of their holes and the entertainment continued. We were friends again. (382)

Reb Shloyme, in *Of Bygone Days*, is described similarly, as studying the Kesalonites as a natural scientist studies mosquitoes, fleas, or frogs (253), and he insists at one point that it is useless for a Jew to write an autobiography as it will lack distinctiveness. 'We are a congregation— no, a heap—of ants. What is true of one is true of the lot. In a book on natural history, you find a chapter on ants, not on any one ant' (259).[23]

The brain of the scientist works at the expense of the lover's heart: Mendele's ignorance of love is apparently shared by Abramowitz. In *The Beggar Book*, Fishke's story of his love for Beila affects Mendele so strongly that he feels that he is going mad: 'Several times I repeated to myself in astonishment: God in heaven! This falling-in-love of man with woman and woman with man—what is it like? I've heard that it occurs, but what it is I do not know' (132). Abramowitz was brought up to regard love as ephemeral (*Of Bygone Days*, 279–80) and marriage as a religious obligation and a business transaction. Both his marriages were arranged, and he hardly knew his wives prior to marriage. In each case, his primary motive appears to have been freedom from financial worry, and he actually refused to marry his second wife, Pessiah Levin, until her father, the lawyer Salman Levin, paid him a 1,000 rouble dowry—an inauspicious start to a fifty-nine year marriage![24]

Mendele and Abramowitz also share a fierce hatred of Jewish communal leaders, whom they usually regard as being corrupt and self-serving. Mendele's disdain for the town 'princes' and 'do-gooders' verges, in his own account, on the pathological. In a remarkable interior monologue in 'Warsaw 1881', Mendele confesses his irrational hatred of authority:

I may be standing gravely with one of the successful do-gooders, who condescends to tell me of his wealth, wisdom, great deeds, charity and goodness. I listen, I believe what he says, my mouth drops open as for summer rain, taking it all in with pleasure. Then a spark of doubt: is he making it all up? And I wonder: what would happen, for example, if I spat in his face? Or if I stroked his cheek, laughing at him: 'Fool! Utter fool!' (427)

[23] On antisemitic elements of caricature in Mendele, as well as parallels in Russian literature, see ch. 3. More recent works in which the Jews are depicted entomologically include Tadeusz Borowski's *This Way to the Gas, Ladies and Gentlemen* (London, 1976 [1959]), and Saul Bellow's *Mr. Sammler's Planet* (London, 1970).

[24] Klausner, *Historia shel hasifrut ha'ivrit hachadashah*, vi. 337.

Similarly, in *The Beggar Book*, Mendele is at one point so incensed against the communal authorities that only with great difficulty does he prevent himself from spewing out his venom and interrupting Fishke's story (129).

Abramowitz's anti-authoritarianism is, perhaps, most vivid in a youthful literary-critical work, *Mishpat shalom* (Judgement of Peace, 1860), which is anything but peaceful. It includes a vicious attack on the Hebrew educator and writer Eliezer Zweifel who, in a collection of essays *Minim ve'ugav* (Strings and Flute, 1858), had condemned the extremism of the Haskalah towards Jewish traditionalists. Abramowitz begins by stating that one should not be influenced by people simply because they are 'authorities' and goes on to carp at Zweifel, mocking and denigrating his work, suggesting at one point that it should be burnt.[25]

At the core of Abramowitz's early literary works—including *The Parasite*, *Fathers and Sons*, *The Tax*, and *The Mare*—is a similarly ferocious hatred of authority. In these works, he satirizes and calls into question the principles, customs, and values of nineteenth-century Russian Jewish society. His *Natural History* does the same by setting science up as the only true authority and implicitly rejecting human authority. Abramowitz's attacks on communal leaders in *The Tax* aroused such anger in Berdichev that his life was threatened, and in these circumstances he and his family left the town in 1869.[26]

Both Mendele and Abramowitz are deeply shocked and changed by the pogroms. In 'Earthquake Days', Mendele describes his consequent sense of alienation from Russia, which he shared with large numbers of Russian Jews at the time.

Everything I saw looked strange: the forests, the fields, had all changed utterly. As if they had stopped living in peace with me and were whispering: 'Not for you, Reb Yid, not for you the trees sway, the grasses glisten, the valleys wrap themselves in grain, the earth gives up its yield; not for you the sound of the turtle-dove, the sweet song of birds; and hills of spices give their aroma, but not for you!' And even the sun, oy! did not warm as before. (406)[27]

---

[25] On Mendele's controversy with Zweifel, with which serious Hebrew literary criticism is thought to have begun, see Morris Neiman, *A Century of Modern Hebrew Literary Criticism, 1784–1884* (New York, 1983), 74 ff. Neiman points out that Mendele's own early criticism was in no way different from Zweifel's *Minim ve'ugav* (78–9).

[26] Klausner, *Historia shel hasifrut ha'ivrit hachadashah*, vi. 350.

[27] An almost identical sense of alienation from nature is felt by Shloyme after his father's death in *Of Bygone Days*; see ch. 5 and the Conclusion.

As for Abramowitz, the pogroms stunned him into a silence which lasted for years and from which he emerged with the revolutionary act of introducing the character of Mendele into Hebrew and by becoming primarily a Hebrew writer. In early 1882, he wrote to his friend, Judah Leib Binstock:

I constantly prepare to write, but cannot begin. My head is clouded with sorrow and depression caused by the pogroms. At the least effort to write, I am threatened with a flood of bitterness. One feels compelled to write, not with ink but with bile and blood. To write this way one must be sure that the body can hold out in so hard an operation. If not, it will burst with emotion. You understand, my friend, no longer be astonished that I have written nothing for so long.[28]

Most strikingly, Mendele is characterized by a lack of dogma and ideology, by volatility or lability of temperament and ambivalence towards himself and others—all true of Abramowitz. In 'Earthquake Days', Mendele confesses that inwardly he is a bundle of conflicts.

I've often felt that there are twin Mendeles struggling inside me, each with his own individuality, constantly bickering and fighting. If one cries, the other laughs; one praises, the other condemns. One Mendele is a fool, he takes everything at face value . . . The other is sharp and sly as a snake; cynic that he is, he knows that not all that glitters is gold. (413–14)

This picture of 'twin Mendeles' in conflict with one another is re-peated in *The Beggar Book* (103). Elsewhere, in 'Warsaw 1881', Mendele admits that the chaos of warring emotions within him is so intense that at times he doubts his sanity.

Sometimes, alone and soul-searching, weighing up my feelings, thoughts and actions, I am so astonished that I doubt my sanity. The mind is home to many forces, each with its function and latent power—its private soul—emerging in a variety of warring emotions. Everything in me has its antithesis. At times the conflicts lie dormant, like the proverbial weasel and cat feasting on the milk of ill-fortune [San. 105*a*]—adversity makes strange bedfellows. At other times they fight each other, tumultuous as in a madhouse, one feeling rapidly changing into another, changing continually in conflict. This is true of all volatile creatures, except that their changeability varies—some at rare inter-vals, others in the space of hours or minutes. I, for my sins, am among the few

---

[28] Letter of 24 Jan./5 Feb. 1882; National Library Archives, Jerusalem. Most of the letters quoted in the present study appear in *Dos Mendele buch* (The Mendele Book), ed N. Mayzel (New York, 1959).

in whom two opposites sometimes co-exist simultaneously. I pass from grief to joy in the flash of an eyelid. (427)[29]

These descriptions of Mendele's inner conflicts and mercuriality are matched by Abramowitz's self-portraits as well as by the reminiscences of friends. As we shall see in the Conclusion, they provide important clues to understanding his depiction of the Jews. In his self-portrait as a young man in *Of Bygone Days*, he is veritably a living ganglion of irreconcilable antagonisms:

No man is spiritually whole, though he might seem to be. Man is multi-faceted. God makes him a bundle of contradictions. But the degree of inner conflict varies. In Shloymele it was pronounced: the god of light and the god of darkness waged constant, indecisive war. Shloymele was both tough and sensitive, hot-tempered and cool-minded, haughty and humble, irascible and compassionate, jokester and thinker, lazy and busy, etc., etc. Shloymele was passionate by nature. The slightest thing would set his heart on fire. (268)

The vignette of the author toward the end of his life in 'The Memory-Book' shows that the child was father to the man, that his inconstancy was consistent.

My temperament, like the weather, is always changing, and in those days [during the Russo-Japanese war of 1904–5] it was particularly variable. A chronic illness, a plague of excited nerves—these are descriptions of such mood changes: from grief to joy, hope to despair, song to lament, love to hate, prayer to obscenity [*mitefilah letiflah*], praise to folly [*mitehilah letohalah*], and vice versa, as the winter wind changes ten times a minute. (372)

The historian Simon Dubnow, who for many years took part in literary meetings with Abramowitz in Odessa, made the following observations on his unstable temperament, accompanied by a total lack of dogma or ideology. 'He never accepted the authority of any dogma or any commonly held view. In a sociological and political sense he was "wild". His views changed with his moods . . . He stood on the side and did not belong to any stream or movement . . . At every meeting he put forward a different opinion.'[30]

Abramowitz's ambivalence towards others is highlighted in his relationship with Ahad Ha'am, whom he both revered and mocked for

[29] On the satiric mixture of laughter and tears in Mendele, see Gershon Shaked, *Bein sechok ledemah: Iyunim bitzirato shel Mendele Mocher Sefarim* (Between Laughter and Tears: Studies in Mendele's Works), (Tel Aviv, 1965).

[30] Simon Dubnow, 'Zikhronot al Mendele Mocher Sefarim' (Reminiscences about Mendele Mocher Sefarim), *Hado'ar*, 4 Apr./14 Nisan (1958 [1918]), 404, 409.

his idea of the revival of the 'Jewish spirit' (*ruach* = 'spirit' or 'wind').
In his view, the 'Jewish spirit' did not need reviving—it was alive and
well. Playing on the liturgical prayer for rain—'He who restores the
wind and makes the rain fall' (*mashiv haruach umorid hagashem*)—he
would ironically call Ahad Ha'am the *mashiv haruach*, implying that he
was a windbag. He is reported by a young acquaintance as saying that
he rejected political Zionism as Judaism is intrinsically Zionistic.

You should know why I am not a Zionist: because the entire Jewish people is
Zionistic. The belief in the coming of the Messiah and the redemption—that
is Zionism . . . I am not a Zionist as God does not dwell in the hearts of the
Zionists! I cannot picture to myself nationalism without religion . . . Our
Judaism is the love of living creatures, humanity and national feeling.[31]

(According to Dubnow, Abramowitz's public stance on Zionism was
owing to his position as headmaster of a Jewish school, for which he
required a government licence.[32]) In contrast, Ahad Ha'am argued
that Judaism and Jewish nationalism were separate. Yet, despite his
antipathy to political Zionism, Abramowitz was a member of Hovevei
Zion, an advocate of Jewish labour in Palestine, and an admirer of
Herzl and Pinsker;[33] and he once compared himself and Ahad Ha'am
to electrical forces driving one another. Typically, he claimed, he was
sometimes so furious at Ahad Ha'am that he would have liked to hang
the philosopher, but after the hanging, 'I myself would have delivered a
bitter eulogy, for who could replace him?'[34]

The reader may have guessed by now that in describing the relationship between Abramowitz and Mendele, I have inadvertently fallen
into the Mendelesque spirit of dialectic: first proving that author and
character are dissimilar, then showing that they are virtually identical.
Mendele's capacity for tolerating contradiction and inner conflict, a
vital part of his self-portrayal as well as of his depiction of the Jews, is
charmingly illustrated in the following anecdote related by the literary
historian and critic Joseph Klausner.

[31] H. L. Gordon, 'Sichah im Mendele Mocher Sefarim' (A Conversation with
Mendele Mocher Sefarim), Kressel Archive, Oxford Centre for Postgraduate Hebrew
Studies, Yarnton, Oxford.
[32] Dubnow, 'Zikhronot', 409.
[33] As an admirer of Pinsker, Mendele translated Pinsker's Zionist tract 'Autoemancipation' into Yiddish (1884). However, he altered Pinsker's text, suggesting instead that
the Land of Israel should become an asylum for Jewish paupers.
[34] Ravnitzky, *Dor vesoferav*, i. 104.

[Moses Leib] Lilienblum [one of the founders of Hibbat Zion] told me that he once attended Rosh Hashana services at the Talmud Torah where Mendele was headmaster [in Odessa]. On the first day, for four hours with a few interruptions for prayer, Mendele proved that all the Jews' troubles were caused by their excessive individualism: lack of discipline, discord, controversy, slander, excessive empty *pilpul* [casuistry], boasting and coquetry, arrogance and self-aggrandisement, stubbornness, etc., etc. When the service was over, Mendele said to Lilienblum: 'Tomorrow during prayer I'll prove the opposite.' And he did. The next day, for four hours with interruptions, the wise old man proved that if not for their individualism the Jews would have perished. They would not have had the spirit to oppose the whole world, to fight for their beliefs, to sacrifice themselves in God's name, to be 'a people that dwells alone, counting for nothing among nations [Num. 23: 9].'[35]

In his fiction, however, Mendele cruelly overemphasizes the flaws of the Jews rather than their achievements, resilience, and creativity. If we have so far considered Mendele as a builder of two literatures and as the creator of the first great character in these literatures, we now turn to the ugly side of Mendele for unrivalled insight not only into the psychology of self-hate among the Jews and among persecuted minorities in general but also into nineteenth-century Russian society.

[35] Klausner, *Historia shel hasifrut ha'ivrit hachadashah*, vi. 435.

3

Antisemitism and Jewish Self-Hate
in Mendele

MENDELE'S fiction evinces a continuous inner struggle between the
scientific observer and the wildly subjective satirist, between personal
and collective love and loathing. His portrayal of the Jews is consistent
with his volatility and cantankerousness and with his unstable self-
image; and as Simon Dubnow recalled, his single glaring fault was 'his
subjective judgement of others. Petty causes could turn him into an
enemy. In conversation with friends, he would pour scorn on many
persons, close and distant alike. I would sometimes tell him off as in
his relationships with others he always saw their negative qualities, not
the positive ones.'[1]

That this subjectivity affected Mendele's perception of the Jews
was clear in his conversation which, J. H. Ravnitzky observed diplo-
matically,

was not bound with the cords of scientific exactitude. It welled up freely with
artistic excitement and poetic exaggeration, depending upon his current impressions and inspiration. So you shouldn't be surprised if a few days previously, he gave the Jews the highest praise—'The world is the book of the
Holy One, blessed be He, and in this book the Congregation of Israel is part of
the poetry, wonderful poetry, God's Song of Songs'—and today he accuses
and attacks the erstwhile 'Chosen People' whose 'divine image' had deserted
them, and he would point to the sickness and filth peculiar to this nation
chosen above all nations, which had made it a disgrace and a horror among the
nations.[2]

Mendele's Jewish self-hate was so strong that brief acquaintances
who caught him at a bad moment could come away convinced that he
was a rabid antisemite. This was apparently the case with the Hebrew
writer S. M. Melamed, who met Mendele in 1906 in Geneva where
the latter had temporarily found refuge from the pogroms. In 1914,

---

[1] Dubnow, 'Zikhronot', 409.   [2] Ravnitzky, *Dor vesoferav* i. 95.

during the controversy over the refusal of the Odessa Hebrew Literary Society to admit Mendele as an honorary member, Melamed recalled this meeting when he spoke out in support of the society.

Mendele, despite his achievement in Hebrew literature, is an extreme assimilationist, a remnant of the Haskalah era, who despises and hates Judaism. This is no exaggeration but a fact. Eight years ago I met him in Geneva and we discussed Jews and Judaism at length. I will never forget the bad impression the old man made on me. He cursed and reviled the Jews not simply as an anti-Semite but like one of the early Gnostics. One who claims that Judaism is nothing but a curse does not deserve to be an honorary member of any Jewish national society.[3]

A number of social and psychological factors strongly affected Mendele's perception of the Jews. There was the problem of having an ancient and clearly defined identity as a religious minority living among a hostile, variegated, and deeply divided non-Jewish majority whose national and cultural identity was not secure. There were also the degrading physical conditions which, as in the case of Job, could lead observers to judge the Jews worthy of their abasement; the Jewish religious tradition of self-blame which (not unlike self-blame among children in troubled or broken families) helps to maintain the illusion of control and stability amid chaos; and the Russian literary tradition of self-criticism, which assumed special importance in the absence of political parties and a free press. There was the bombshell of Darwin's doctrine of natural selection, which was often taken to justify racism and the idea that might makes right, and which Mendele must have pondered deeply during the 1860s when his major work was *Natural History*. There was also the desire among Haskalah writers to defeat or escape the narrowness of traditional Judaism and, at the same time, to achieve government approval by presenting a negative view in line with official, or semi-official, policy. To this must be added the inhibiting effect of government censorship, which was more partial to criticism of the Jews than, say, to the assertion of Jewish national pride.

Overshadowing all this was antisemitism, both religious and racist, which blocked the path to emancipation and tainted many Russian

---

[3] S. M. Melamed, *Hamitzpeh*, 11/19 (8 May 1914); Kressel Archive, Oxford Centre for Postgraduate Hebrew Studies, Yarnton, Oxford. For a recent study of Jewish self-hatred (although without mention of Mendele) see Sander L. Gilman, *Jewish Self-Hatred: Anti-Semitism and the Hidden Language of the Jews* (Baltimore, 1986).

Jewish intellectuals of the time with self-hate,[4] which was probably exacerbated by the self-loathing common among enlightened Russians in the nineteenth century. In the context of the history of antisemitism, Mendele's fiction evolved in two distinct stages: the creation of the Yiddish character of Mendele the Bookpeddler during the antisemitic backlash to the Polish revolt of 1863; and the introduction of Mendele into Hebrew fiction after the pogroms of 1881–4. Perhaps more clearly than any other work written by a Jew in tsarist Russia, *The Mare* sets out the limits, conditions, and conflicts involved in being a Jewish writer at the time. On the one hand, *The Mare*, despite its allegorical form, is a most forceful and courageous attack on antisemitism, on the Pale of Settlement and the restrictions of Jewish life within the Pale (e.g. 311, 332); on violence against the Jews (337, 344); on the antisemitic press (345); on antisemitic discrimination in educational institutions (320); on prejudices which hold the Jews to be parasites (312), subhuman, and lacking souls (ibid.), and, above all, Christ-killers (335). It is not surprising that, alone among Mendele's works, *The Mare* got Mendele into trouble with the Russian police.[5] On the other hand—the attack on antisemitism is put into the mouth of the Devil! Specific blame for the conditions of the Jews, as symbolized by the mare, is overwhelmingly attached to the Jews themselves (327, 333, 334–5, 346 ff.). At one point, the mare gives a whole catalogue of its exploiters and oppressors, all of whom are Jews (327).

It is impossible, then, to forget when reading Mendele that he lived in the most reactionary and backward empire of the time, where Jews until the revolution were hedged in with countless restrictions and were officially classed as aliens (*inorodtsy*, 'those of the other race'). The historian Bernard Lewis has written that in its antisemitism, Russia was exceptional even in a predominantly antisemitic European milieu.

Despite the volume and vehemence of anti-Semitic literature in nineteenth and early-twentieth century Europe, with one exception, it did no more than delay the advance of Jewish emancipation, and left nothing worse than some

---

[4] See Leon Poliakov, *The History of Antisemitism*, vol. iii, *From Voltaire to Wagner* (London, 1975), 259 ff. Perhaps the most pernicious antisemitic publications in Russia prior to the *Protocols of the Elders of Zion* were written by a converted Jew, Jacob Brafman. For a bibliography on antisemitism in Russia see Gershon David Hundert and Gershon C. Bacon, *The Jews in Poland and Russia: Bibliographical Essays* (Bloomington, Ind., 1984), 170–4.

[5] Klausner, *Historia shel hasifrut ha'ivrit hachadashah*, vi. 358.

remaining educational, professional and social barriers. The one exception was the empire of the czars, where the ideas of the theoreticians of anti-Semitism were given both wider circulation and more practical effect.[6]

A hundred years later, most Jews living in the West can take their freedoms for granted, but for Mendele the only 'free country' was the bath-house.

> The bath-house for the Jew is a motherland, a free country. Great and small alike can air their views there. Anyone can rise to the highest position and take courage in his misery, cast off his worries and troubles and find rest—an hour of peace of mind. (*The Travels of Benjamin the Third*, 83)

Under tsarist rule, a strong element of distortion, bias, and self-hate was almost inevitable among Jewish writers. In *The Hebrew Novel in Czarist Russia*, David Patterson describes the conflicts inherent in being a Hebrew novelist at the time.

> The social aspects of the novels reflect the ambivalent attitude of many of the authors under review, the love–hate relationship which they display towards the Jewish people, and the simultaneous loyalty and revulsion which they evince in the face of the dreadful plight of the communities of eastern Europe. The genuine desire to ease their people's burden becomes all the more poignant in the light of their inability to suggest any but peripheral remedies, and of their helplessness in the face of problems of such magnitude. In spite of their passionate involvement, and the deep sincerity which characterizes their strictures against the social abuses of their time, thereby lending a measure of power and conviction to their stories, the very ardour of their plea often tends to exaggerate and distort the picture of the society they portray, so that considerable caution must be exercised before accepting their depiction of Jewish life at its face value. For all the elements of realism, which may be detected so frequently within these novels, it is important to recall that the facts of the society they portray are presented through the prism of the various attitudes adopted by the novelists to their environment—attitudes which may be heavily weighted in accordance with a preconceived and highly prejudiced point of view. Indeed, in some respects their portraits—certainly the most virulent amongst them—shed more light at times upon their own states of mind than upon the state of the society they describe.[7]

---

[6] Bernard Lewis, *Semites and Anti-Semites: An Inquiry into Conflict and Prejudice* (London, 1986), 96.

[7] David Patterson, *The Hebrew Novel in Czarist Russia* (Edinburgh, 1964), 221. These observations are equally true of other contemporary writers, Yiddish as well as Hebrew, who may have influenced Mendele, such as Isaac Meir Dick, Isaac Kaminer, and Joseph Brill.

Russian literature was not much different in its distortions, for it was full of antisemitic stereotyping in its mainstream:[8] Lermontov's play *The Spaniards*, Turgenev's story 'The Jew', Gogol's novel *Taras Bulba*, Dostoyevsky's fictional memoir *The House of the Dead*, the satires of Saltykov-Shchedrin, Tolstoy's *Anna Karenina*, among others, betray the shameful prejudice and hatred nourished by the Church and kept alive in the popular imagination. All these writers influenced Mendele to a greater or lesser extent. Interestingly, when Russian literature began for the first time, in a liberal backlash to the pogroms of 1881–4 (and, later, to those of 1903–6), to depict Jews favourably—for example, in works by Leskov, Chekhov, Korolenko, and Gorky—Mendele and other Jewish writers began to depict the Jews in a markedly less satirical and more realistic and sympathetic vein.

It is important to emphasize, too, that Russian literature is itself punctuated with self-loathing; as Bazarov puts it succinctly in Turgenev's *Fathers and Sons*, 'The only good thing about a Russian is the poor opinion he has of himself.'[9] This poor opinion, Turgenev implies, is fully justified. Isaiah Berlin elaborates in his capsule account of the background to *Fathers and Sons*.

In a huge and backward country, where the number of educated persons was very small and was divided by a gulf from the vast majority of their fellow-men—they could scarcely be described as citizens—living in conditions of unspeakable poverty, oppression, and ignorance, a major crisis of public conscience was bound sooner or later to arise. The facts are familiar enough: the Napoleonic wars precipitated Russia into Europe, and thereby, inevitably, into a more direct contact with Western Enlightenment than had previously been permitted. Army officers drawn from the land-owning elite were brought into a degree of companionship with their men, lifted as they all were by a common wave of vast patriotic emotion. This for the moment broke through the rigid stratification of Russian society. The salient features of this society included an ignorant, State-dominated, largely corrupt church; a small, semi-Westernized, ill-trained bureaucracy struggling to keep back an enormous, primitive, socially and economically undeveloped, semi-feudal, but vigorous and potentially undisciplined, population straining against its shackles; a widespread sense of inferiority, both social and intellectual, before Western civilization; a society distorted by arbitrary bullying from above and nauseating conformity from below, in which men with any degree of independence or originality or character found scarcely any outlet for normal development.[10]

---

[8] See Joshua Kunitz, *Russian Literature and the Jew* (New York, 1929).

[9] Ivan Turgenev, *Fathers and Sons* (1861), tr. R. Edmonds, Penguin edn. (Harmondsworth, Middx., 1965), 116.   [10] Ibid., Isaiah Berlin, Introd., 11–12.

The oppressive yoke of this totalitarian regime was felt by most of the great Russian writers who agitated for reform: Pushkin was virtually under arrest by Nicholas I, all of Ostrovsky's early plays were banned, Saltykov-Shchedrin was exiled for writing a story which condemned social injustice, Turgenev was kept under surveillance after the publication of his *Notes of a Huntsman*, Dostoyevsky spent several years in Siberia, Tolstoy was excommunicated.

Russia's weaknesses were betrayed in its perception and treatment of the Jews and in the Jews' vulnerability. It is a lesson of history that a nation's Jewish policy is a gauge of its self-image. The psychologist Erik Erikson has described how individuals belonging to a hated minority might in any case come to hate their own people: 'The individual belonging to an oppressed and exploited minority, which is aware of the dominant cultural ideals but prevented from emulating them, is apt to fuse the negative images held up to him by the dominant majority with the negative identity cultivated in his own group.'[11] These 'negative images' are likely to be all the more vicious if the dominant majority has a strongly negative self-image. Indeed, it is striking how the main criticisms of Russia by Russian writers are echoed in Haskalah literature and in Mendele's depiction of the Jews: for example, in the charges of the lack of dignity, parasitism, backwardness, and demonic corruption. In his letter to Gogol, Belinsky writes that what Russia needs is 'the reawakening in the people of a sense of their human dignity lost for so many centuries amid the dirt and refuse.'[12] A similar attitude prevailed among enlightened Jews toward the Jewish masses in the Pale of Settlement. In *Dead Souls*, likewise, the charge of parasitism is implicitly levelled by Gogol against the privileged classes, the landowners and the bureaucracy who treat human beings like property. Identical charges against the Jewish upper class appear frequently in nineteenth-century Yiddish and Hebrew literature (for example, in Mendele's *The Parasite*). The critic Chernyshevsky's attack in the 1840s upon the total lack of originality in Russian intellectual life—'What have the Russians given to learning?

[11] Erik Erikson, *Identity: Youth and Crisis* (London, 1974), 303. As we have seen in ch. 1, the Jewish memory of past triumph amid present degradation would have inclined then even further to self-chastisement, if not self-hatred. In this respect, the Jews might be compared with the Arabs, whom Arab critics have often vehemently accused, in language not unlike that used by 19th cent. *maskilim*, of decline, backwardness, and fossilization, with the aim of awakening the Arab mind from its medieval slumber to regain its medieval glory. See Raphael Patai, *The Arab Mind* (New York, 1983), 247–67.

[12] Vissarion Belinsky, *Selected Philosophical Works* (Westport, 1981), 537.

Alas, nothing. What has learning contributed to Russian life? Again, nothing'[13]—is echoed in the critique of traditional Jewish life in Haskalah literature. Turgenev went so far in his novel *Smoke* as to suggest that if Russia were destroyed it would be no great loss to civilization.

Even the idea that the Jews are in some way possessed by the Devil, in *The Mare* as in the traditional anti-Jewish stereotype, is echoed in the sad and moving description of Russia at the end of Dostoyevsky's *The Possessed*, published in 1871–2, not long before *The Mare*. Shortly before his death, the aged progressive scholar Stepan Verhovensky retells the New Testament story of the devils entering the swine as a parable of contemporary Russia: 'that's exactly like our Russia, those devils that come out of the sick man and enter into the swine. They are all the sores, all the foul contagions, all the impurities, all the devils great and small that have multiplied in that great invalid, our beloved Russia, in the course of ages and ages.'[14]

Not surprisingly, then, Russia's leading satirist of the late nineteenth century, Saltykov-Shchedrin, who influenced Mendele in his satiric portrayal of towns such as Glupsk and in beast fables such as *The Mare*—he used the battered mare as a symbol of the exploited Russian peasant—took a deeply negative view of Russian society and institutions, which he characterized as being ruled by 'arbitrariness, hypocrisy, lying, rapacity, and vacuity'.[15]

The general conditions of the Russian peasant—the majority of Russian society—at the time of the emancipation of the serfs in 1861, moreover, were not far different from those of the Jews.

The country's fifty-two million peasants knew only the most primitive agricultural techniques at the time of their emancipation. They knew next to nothing about sanitation, public health, or personal hygiene. They lived in a world peopled by demons, ghosts, elves, and other spectral creatures, whose interventions were used to explain bad luck, good fortune, prosperity, life, and death. Almost none of them was literate, and therefore they were effectively cut off from the country in which they lived. Newspapers, the only means of communication available in the nineteenth century, could have no impact upon them, nor could they be instructed by them. In the entire Russian Empire, not

[13] Quoted in Donald W. Treadgold, *The West in Russia and China*, vol. i. *Russia, 1472–1917* (Cambridge, 1973), 181.

[14] Tr. Constance Garnett, 2 vols. (London, 1952), ii. 288.

[15] Quoted by I. P. Foote, Introduction to M. Saltykov-Shchedrin, *The Golovlets* (New York, 1986 [1875–80]), p. vii.

more than 350,000 children out of a total population of 75,000,000 were attending any sort of school at the time of Alexander II's accession [1855].[16]

Yet, if the life of the Russian peasant was grim, the life of the Russian Jew was made harder by antisemitic laws. During a period of about 120 years, approximately 140 restrictive laws were passed against the Jews by the Russian government;[17] while not always effective, these laws curtailed the Jews economically and socially, as well as geographically, and made them aliens in their country of birth. Russian antisemitism provided fertile soil for the growth of Jewish self-hatred, especially among the *maskilim*, who were painfully aware of the abject Jewish condition, often at odds with Jewish society, and more strongly conscious than most Russian Jews that in theory their social handicaps could be cast aside by abdicating their religion and gaining their entrance ticket to European civilization—the Jew was granted full legal equality as soon as he changed his religion.[18]

Especially during the tyrannical age of Nicholas I (1825–55), when Mendele was growing up, the Jews sank to unprecedented poverty and degradation. Although five of Mendele's seven novels are set in this time, they do not, and cannot, blame the government openly for the persecution of the Jews and give barely an inkling of the legislative background to this persecution. These laws were clear and infinitely disturbing signs of a Russian social malaise and causes of Jewish self-hate. Apart from the relentless poverty, the greatest suffering was caused by the laws of 1827 obliging Jewish communities to fill a quota of conscripts ('cantonists') between the ages of 12 and 25 for twenty-five years' military service starting from age 18. The six 'preparatory' years were intended solely to cause suffering to the Jews by breaking up their families and pressuring the child-conscripts to convert to Christianity; it is noteworthy that of the 84,536 Jewish conversions to Christianity in nineteenth-century Russia, the majority were under one form or another of coercion.[19] The recruitment laws turned Jew against Jew, divided rich and poor, and created a breed of communal official (*khappers*, or 'snatchers') whose awful job it was to fill the

---

[16] W. Bruce Lincoln, *The Romanovs: Autocrats of All the Russias* (London, 1981), 507. On the conditions of the Russian Jews, see ch. 4 below.

[17] Alexis Goldenweiser, 'Legal Status of the Jews in Russia', in J. Frumkin *et al.* (eds.), *Russian Jewry (1860–1917)*, tr. M. Ginsburg (London, 1966), 85.

[18] Ibid. 86.

[19] Paul Mendes-Flohr and Judah Reinharz (eds.), *The Jew in the Modern World: A Documentary History* (New York, 1980), 539.

quotas. Often this was done cruelly, with young children of the very poor.

Whereas in all Western European lands military conscription for the Jews was a stage towards or accompanied their emancipation, the reverse was true in Russia. Dozens of discriminatory laws followed the laws of 1827, making the position of the Jews increasingly untenable. They lived in fear of expulsion; this, in fact, happened to the Jews of Kiev in 1835. They were severely limited in their rights of residence and choice of profession. They were burdened with higher taxes than the general population. Their communal organization, the *kahal*, was by 1844 stripped of its autonomy. Blood libels were not uncommon. By a law of 1851, Jewish men were prohibited from wearing traditional clothes and earlocks, and the women were forbidden to shave their heads after marriage; the police were empowered to enforce these and many other degrading laws, and for the most part did so. Most sinister of all was a law of 1851 which divided the Jews into 'useful' (merchants, artisans, professionals, etc.) and 'useless' (petty traders, paupers, etc.): the 'useless' Jews were the vast majority. The Crimean War marked the nadir of Russian Jewish life before the pogroms. A law of 1853 entitled Jews to seize other Jews absent from their places of residence without passports and give them up as substitute recruits or for cash. (Benjamin and Senderel in *The Travels of Benjamin the Third* are victims of this law.) Yet, for all their suffering, the Jews among whom Mendele was born and came to maturity had neither the education nor the self-confidence to agitate politically for the improvement of their lot. The historian W. Bruce Lincoln, in his biography of Nicholas I, has pointed out that whereas other minorities, especially the Ukrainians, were susceptible to anti-Russian propaganda during the upheavals of 1848, 'the most oppressed minority of all, the Jews, remained largely passive. It is one of the ironies of Russian history that a minority so incessantly persecuted and so unjustly treated by imperial officials, remained basically loyal to the imperial government until late in the 19th century.'[20]

Especially during the first half of the nineteenth century, when it was government policy to encourage conversion among the Jews, Russian antisemitic legislation was designed to make the Jews hate being Jews. Yet, Mendele's self-hate was relatively mild, based as it

[20] W. Bruce Lincoln, *Nicholas I. Emperor and Autocrat of All the Russias*, Penguin edn. (Harmondsworth, Middx., 1978), 289.

was upon circumstances rather than on religious or socio-political ideology. It shunned the Church stereotype of the Jews as Christ killers, well-poisoners, or blood-sucking money-lenders, and it had no truck with the more recent racism which held the Jews to be secret diabolical conspirers to rule the world, a destructive biological evil which must be eradicated. Expressed through satire, Mendele's self-hate had a healthy side, as a sign of concern and a spur to change, and his self-mockery was virtually a condition of survival in the Pale of Settlement.

It is a striking fact, nevertheless, that while there are numerous Jewish villains in Mendele's stories, there are no Christian villains, not even in the stories set against the pogroms; and while the virtues of individual Jews are exceptional, their villainies are treated as a collective Jewish aberration. Similarly, the extraordinary efforts of the Russian Jews to improve their lives are largely ignored by Mendele: for example, their vital role in the creation of the Zionist movement; in the growth of the socialist and revolutionary movements; in the establishment of countless charities and self-help organizations, of which the best known is ORT; in the mass emigrations of 1881–1914. In fact, Mendele expressed contempt for the panic-stricken Jews who fled Russia during the pogroms. 'The Jew always was, is, and will be a submissive cow giving milk, or a "miserable beast of burden". He'll go, whether to America or to Palestine, and he'll remain a beast of burden.'[21] Mendele often calls up the physical stereotype of the Jews in grim reminders that physique and physiognomy were often linked at the time with moral character and that the idea of inherited criminality was common prior to the First World War. However, the image of physical decrepitude among the Jews was all too real. Their meagre diet, physically wearing existence, and the grind of persecution took their toll. A study by the Russian War Department in 1875 found that twice as many Jews were deficient physically as non-Jews, and recruiting records that year showed that over twice as many Jews were physically unfit for military service.[22] For this reason, Mendele's

---

[21] Letter to Judah Leib Binstock, 11/23 Apr. 1882; National Library Archives, Jerusalem. Cf. J. L. Gordon's poem 'Eder Adonai' (Flock of God), written at the same time.

[22] Louis Stanley Greenberg, *The Jews in Russia: The Struggle for Emancipation* (New Haven, Conn., 1965), i. 164. While the effects of inbreeding and a propensity to malinger may have increased the number of Jews unfit for military service recorded in the Russian recruitment statistics, the main causes of their physical decrepitude were hardship and poor diet.

caricature of the Jews treads a perilous line between realism and pathos, entertainment and bad taste.

Mendele was not unaware of his problems and responsibilities as a satirist and had sharp insight into the psychology of antisemitism and self-hate. In an 1875 essay, he denounces the failure of non-Jews to regard Jews as individuals. 'It has been clear for some time that the nations regard "the Jews" collectively. They do not distinguish one Jew from another as a distinct personality but group them together like sheep or cattle: if Tuviah is to blame, Zigud must be too [Pes. 113*b*].'[23] In an essay of 1878, he again quotes from the Talmud to illustrate the mechanism of projection. 'Every nation charges others with its faults [Kid. 70*a*] and is blind to the precious aphorism, "before you tell another to take the splinter from his teeth, take the beam from your own eye" [*Bava Batra* 15*b*].'[24] Mendele's sensitive awareness of the pathological origins and vile character of prejudice seems to have had little effect upon his portrayal of the Jews, the ugliness of which is cumulatively overwhelming. He himself employs countless times the same techniques of generalization and projection which he decries in gentile attitudes towards the Jews. Though he accuses 'the nations' for not distinguishing one Jew from another, he does exactly the same, time and again returning to the alleged uniformity of the Jews, sneering at them as 'limbs of one body attached to and dependent on each other . . . like the sick, afflicted limbs of Israel's body' (446, 447), mocking them as cucumbers or pickled herrings, all alike, packed together (214), prolific as mushrooms in the dark or potatoes in a filthy cellar (97, 412). In 'The Fire-Victims', an indigent Kesalonite complains to Mendele that the house of study where he slept has burnt down in a fire which destroyed the whole town—this often happened in Russia—and Mendele cruelly remarks to himself: 'Fleas if they could talk would argue so after losing their lodging in houses and beds' (445). *Of Bygone Days* contains Mendele's most idiosyncratic attack on this uniformity, again using insect imagery.

Is there another people in the whole world whose life from birth to death follows the same pattern? The upbringing of the Jew, his education, his prayers and *piyutim* with their formulae and melodies—everything has a fixed style, even the rules of eating and drinking are the same everywhere. Has there ever

[23] Shalom Ya'akov Abramowitz, 'Hagoy lo nikhsaf' (Shameless nation), *Hamagid*, 19/20 (1875), 173.

[24] Id., 'Ahavah le'umit vetoledotelliah' (Nationalism and Its Consequences), *Hamelitz*, 14/6 (1878), col. 117.

been anything like it? Friday nights, for instance, Jews all over the world eat fish, noodles and vegetables with bread. On Sabbath they eat radishes, horse-radish, leg-and-liver gravy with onions, egg and dried rice with a great hollow bone. One day—pancakes, another day—bagels and bread in dumplings and sesame seeds, a third day—chollah with saffron, gold-plaited. When a Jew in Spain blesses the Sabbath or fasts on Yom Kippur, his prayers echo across the ocean as far away as Argentina. We are a congregation—no, a heap—of ants. In a book on natural history you find a chapter on ants, not on any one ant. (259)[25]

Similarly, in *The Beggar Book*, when Mendele classifies the species of Jewish beggar—the list is endless and even includes bookselling!— Reb Alter, exasperated, breaks in: 'I've had enough of your beggars! It makes me itch just to hear of them, as if a crowd of fleas have attacked me. You should make it short and sweet: the Jews are beggars, and have done with it' (115).

It was a bitter irony that the decline of religious faith and the elevation of science, which Mendele supported enthusiastically in the first half of his career, could lead logically to so low a perception of human beings. As an assiduous student of natural science, Mendele was influenced, as we have seen, by Darwin's doctrine of natural selection which in distorted form, Jacob Talmon has written, 'brought down one of the strongest barriers protecting "Thou shalt not kill"'.[26] Mendele's attacks on Jewish uniformity are little different from the contemptuous views of people expressed by Bazarov in Turgenev's *Fathers and Sons*: 'no botanist would dream of studying each individual birch-tree'.[27]

Mendele does not just caricature the Jews, he portrays them as caricatures of human beings—semi-starved, over-crowded, persecuted. Mendele the Bookpeddler himself does trade with their sufferings, selling them religious books for weeping and mourning (91). They are little better than serfs, 'live merchandise' (145, 161), their value to one another being exclusively economic. The children of the very poor were most often exploited as servants, prostitutes, or cannon-fodder and reduced to a subhuman state: 'Can children of the poor be described as human?' (76); 'Can a poor girl, hired for bread, be called a human being?' (148). This dehumanization may be seen as the

---

[25] Mendele the Bookpeddler, too, describes the Jews as being ant-like; see pp. 41–2 above.

[26] Jacob Talmon, 'European History as the Seedbed of the Holocaust', in J Sonntag (ed.), *Jewish Perspectives: Twenty-five Years of Modern Jewish Writing* (London, 1980), 14.

[27] Turgenev, *Fathers and Sons*, 160.

essence of Mendele's satire.[28] Blatant antisemitic stereotyping occurs in Mendele's description of the typical Jewish nose, 'long, humped, slanting to a sharp tip' (389). Elsewhere he declares that 'of every ten long Jewish noses created, the Kesalon agents took nine' (189). Even an assimilated Jew, he intimates, is betrayed by the stench of onions and garlic on his breath (442). The Jew is ugly—'There's no need to judge the body of a Jew by aesthetic standards. This is not his lot. His beauty lies in his Jewishness' (427)—and though dirty and unkempt, he paradoxically takes pride in the way he looks: 'The Kesalonite, coat stained with kugel grease, rice, eggyolk, pus, snot, etc. has done no wrong. Contrariwise. The stain is an ornament, proof that he puts on no airs, gives his mind to no idle matters' (378). For Mendele, the Jew is unhygienic and has disgusting manners: 'watch out for the Jew with hand on nose—if you don't, you'll have to rush home to wash your coat' (441). A 'Jewish' town is filthy by definition, admittedly though echoing the frequent criticisms of 'Russian' towns in Russian literature: 'Hirshl wasn't all that surprised at the slops and sewage running in the streets: Kesalon was, after all, a Jewish town' (164).[29] Mendele even calls up the old stereotype of the money-worshipping Jew: 'This is the way the Jews are by nature and have always been. When they see a gold coin—it makes no difference who or what has it—it might even be a calf, an animal in human form—this becomes a god, they dance round it, bow to it and worship it' (391).

Mendele pins 'the Jew' or 'the Jews' to countless other generalizations. 'The Jew is never in time: he eats and drinks at the wrong time, he pays his debts, makes requests, scrutinizes his deeds too late; he marries, has children and grows old too soon' (414). The Jew 'does not propose an idea without degrading everything else' (435). The Jew 'meddles in the personal affairs of his friend' (95). 'The Jew is pushed—so he pushes' (441). The Jews are like Diogenes—head in the clouds, body in a barrel (259). 'No other people is so active in the worship of God, morning to night, as the Jews' (431). 'Only among the Jews can a man sit in a yeshivah all his life and ignore the world around

[28] For an eloquent discussion of this dehumanization as material for Mendele's satires, see Shaked, *Bein sechok ledemah*.

[29] In Gogol's *The Inspector General*, the mayor declares that the town must be cleaned up in every sense before the inspector arrives: 'The more destruction there is everywhere, the more it shows the activity of the town authorities. Ah, I forgot that beside that fence there is a rubbish heap it would take forty wagons to move. What a filthy town it is, to be sure!' See Nikolai Gogol, *The Inspector General*, in *The Collected Tales and Plays of Nikolai Gogol*, ed. L. J. Kent, tr. C. Garnett (New York, 1969), 611.

him . . . Only among the Jews can a man sit in one place with his head in Spain' (272). 'Great is the power of shame among the Jews, making them stubborn, overcoming love, hard as death' (227). The Jews engage in argument for the sake of sharpening the mind as a mouse chews an inedible object to sharpen its teeth (393). The Jews move peculiarly, like poisoned mice (77). 'There is no *mitzvah* which ordinary Jews fulfil with such joy and desire, and so willingly, as giving advice to others to their disadvantage' (440). The Jews 'are prohibited from laughing in this world' (301). The Jew is not authorized to enjoy nature (279). 'Sexual love never existed among the Jews' (ibid.). 'Sweat was created for the Jews. No Jew can have his sabbaths and festivals unless he sweats all over. What people struggle and sweat in this world like the Jews? (93)'. The Jew has little self-respect: 'From the moment he climbs into the wagon, the Jew makes his body public property, a doormat for everyone to tread on' (253). The Jew is devious—'The Jew's custom is to enter in stealth, bent, submissive, quiet; then he springs bear-like from the dust, as it were, to ambush the master of the house' (254).

The Jew is weak, cowardly, passive. Mendele, attacked during a pogrom, can only shout 'Like a Jew, whose sole power lies in his mouth' (383). In *The Travels of Benjamin the Third*, the Jews are mocked for their Oblomov-like passivity, which is supported by their faith. The absence of lighting, the poor roadworks, the filth in the river of Kesalon, must be preserved as they have always existed: 'What heaven decrees must not be annulled' (78). (As a satire on authority both divine and human, *The Travels* with its town of Kesalon/Glupsk (Foolsville) is directly influenced by Saltykov-Shchedrin's Glupov (also Foolsville) in *A History of a Town*.) Benjamin justifies boat travel because his namesake, the medieval traveller Benjamin of Tudela, went by sea. To which Senderel replies: 'If Reb Benjamin of long ago had flown on a broomstick we would certainly have to do the same' (79). The essence of Jewish identity is found in this very passive conservatism which, carried to logical extreme, prefers weakness to strength, sickness to health. Thus, when the little boy in 'The Calf' spends a summer tending a calf in the fields with the result that his physique and appetite improve dramatically, his mother is appalled.

What will become of you? Look at you. You've turned into another man! You no longer look like a Jew. Your face was pale and pleasant once, now it's gross and red. You've put on weight, you're as healthy as Esau. You don't eat like a Jew, bit by bit, but heartily, swallowing a whole chunk of bread at once. That's what you get for tramping each day through the fields and forests. Don't you want to be a normal man? (359)

Jewishness is thus equated with degradation, poverty, and weakness; and this was so especially after the pogroms of 1881, Mendele suggests with biting sarcasm in 'Earthquake Days'.

At such times, when Jewishness is in demand, Leib the *melamed*, a total Jew in every way, is far more able than I to fill this demand. It suits a man like him to stretch his hand out and demand what is rightfully his—charity, that is— because he is so completely Jewish. (407)

Later in the story, Mendele elaborates on this natural right of the Jews, to beg. 'The Jew is not entitled to stand on his dignity. Head bent, he seeks whoever might help him, demands and nags until it is impossible to send him away emptyhanded' (412).

The logic by which being Jewish is equal to being a beggar is pushed to its extreme and twisted paradoxically in 'Shem and Japheth in the Train'. In this story, the man who is travelling with the Jewish family turns out to be a Christian tailor exiled from Prussia in the late 1870s as a Polish national. Although previously an antisemite, he discovers with the help of his Jewish friend that he can best survive by learning Jewish ways, by becoming a Jew in all but religion.

At first it was hard for him, this pupil, to stand up to the trial, and he would rather have died suddenly than live a life so full of toil and trouble and the peculiar afflictions of our people. Slowly, however, he got used to it. In the end, he completed his studies in Beggary, Patience, Submissiveness, Degrada- tion, Torture of Body and Soul, like a fully qualified Jew. From now on, he was ready for *galut* [exile], trained to accept lovingly its suffering and misfortune. (405)

Other metaphors of Jewish existence used by Mendele expand the portrait of passive submission and deformity: an exploited maidservant (310), an immobile orangutang (335), a hunchback (412), a slave (431), a broken mare.

Another element of the stereotype sets Jewish ineffectuality against gentile competence: for example, while gentiles push their wagon out of the mud, Alter and Mendele 'groaned and shuddered all over, as if we ourselves were pushing' (92); when Benjamin is lost while practis- ing to be an explorer in the vicinity of his hometown Batlon, he is saved by a peasant (61–2); and in 'The Festival of Gathering', while the gentiles gather the harvest, the Jews can only gather alms (454).

Humble though they are with gentiles, the Jews treat one another with contempt (335, 380, 421). In *The Beggar Book*, Mendele, having collided with Alter, is afraid at first that a gentile is involved. But when he climbs down from his wagon and sees a bearded Jew, with *tallit* and *tefillin*, he takes heart: 'there's no need to worry' (92). In business dealings particularly, the Jews are described as being unscrupulous towards one another. 'Things of this sort are common among the Jews: two sides cheat one another, they don't fulfil what they undertake, neither is happy with the other. Still, they continue to live together, and their relationship goes on' (354).

Mendele's stereotypic portrayals of Jews often contradict one another. For example, he mocks their passivity but also their almost desperate haste and pushiness. These characteristics, he writes in *In the Valley of Tears*, are present from birth.

The human custom that the soul waits in the heavenly treasure house until a place to live, utensils and the things it needs are ready for it—whereupon it is invited to take a physical form—is impossible for the Jewish soul. A Jew, if not quick to push himself with all his might, if he waits for his place on earth, will never be born, to be sure. But once pushed out among the living, he continues to be pushed, with God's help, on and on; he pushes and pushes with all his strength, he bursts in through doors or windows, front or rear, it's all the same. And so his entire life pushes on, and he doesn't feel a thing. (145)

Elsewhere, the Jews are as pushy as panicked fugitives from a fire or armed thieves.

It's not the sound of panic in a fire or of fugitives from armed thieves—it's just the Jews on their way to the Kesalon train station. Our Jewish brethren race in alarm, bundles bouncing on arms and shoulders, and their women run too, wallowing in pillows and cushions, babies screaming, everyone shoving, shouldering, elbowing up the stairs of the third-class carriage, risking life and limb to capture a seat. (399)

The worst of all, apparently, are the Warsaw Jews, flying madly about like catapult stones and arrows. In one of the surreal incidents which befall Mendele in Warsaw, 'two Jews rushed at me, one from the front turning me right, the other from the rear turning me left, spinning me round like a wheel. Miraculously, the three of us didn't crumble into a heap of bones' (441).

Never far from the surface of this caricature is an almost murderous rage, emerging most clearly in a remarkable passage in 'Shelter from the Storm', when Mendele is overcome by the forced joy of the Jews praying on Shavuot (Pentecost).

> Had I been with the psalmist by the waters of Babylon, I would have taken one of the harps from the willow trees and sung to our infants, a joyful song mixed with such poisonous misery as to drive them mad and, in a wild dance of agony, dash themselves on the rock. (384)

Mendele attaches the most horrifying curse in the Bible to the Jews:

> O daughter of Babylon, you devastator!
> Happy shall be he who requites you
>   with what you have done to us!
> Happy shall be he who takes your little ones
>   and dashes them against the rock!
>
> Ps. 137: 8–9

Bearing in mind Mendele's intensely subjective and volatile temperament, this impulse to destroy must be regarded as a temporary aberration, perhaps (as we shall see in the Conclusion) a projection of his own somewhat distorted self-image. Yet, it might be argued that this curse also flashes out a horrifying truth about Jewish life in eastern Europe. Jewish self-hate and the submission to the 'negative image' created by antisemitism attenuated the will to survive. While the Jewish self-image was primarily positive and resilient, it was apparently not devoid of a suicidal element, encouraging unconscious collusion with the executioner, making the Jews riper for extermination. For if a champion of affirmative Jewish social change such as Mendele could be possessed with such murderous rage against his own people, one can begin to imagine the lust to destroy which seized the enemies of the Jews. There is little doubt, at any rate, that in the history of antisemitism the tsarist maltreatment of the Jews in some ways foreshadowed the Holocaust, that the path to Auschwitz may be glimpsed, albeit in the far distance, in the legislation of Nicholas I.

In general, however, Mendele aims to destroy not the Jews but their poverty and weakness. He never loses sight of the social and economic forces underlying self-hate, nor does he entirely abandon hope that the removal of Jewish disabilities will lead to the elimination of the deformities in their national character. This reform was to be achieved through Haskalah, through education and gradual assimilation into Russian society, though without sacrificing the cardinal beliefs and customs of traditional Judaism. Mendele's struggle for change and his disillusionment with Haskalah are the subject of the next chapter.

4

Mendele's Realism and the Struggle for Change

MUCH of Mendele's satire is intended to promote reforms of various kinds among the Russian Jews, though after 1881 his didacticism takes second place to art. The main goals of the Haskalah movement were those of liberal reformers throughout Europe. These included: political change and basic civil rights for all citizens; educational reform, particularly the creation of a varied secular education; marital reform and the end of child marriage; religious reform, wiping out superstition and reducing oppressive religious authority; reforms in public hygiene and health care; improvements in the lot of children and women and the introduction of such basic women's rights as the right to choose their own husbands; and finally, ideas which had gained widespread currency through the Romantic movement, such as the importance of liberty, nature, childhood, and love. All these and other hoped-for reforms are often described or alluded to satirically in Mendele's fiction. His roles as social reformer and satirist were thus, in fact, two aspects of the same role.

For all its constructive, humanistic aims, the Haskalah has been stigmatized as a movement which failed: the pogroms of 1881–4 made clear that the Jews were unlikely to gain emancipation under tsarist rule, and that the Haskalah was out of step with the times as a progressive movement in a reactionary era. Yet, the *maskilim* were the first modern Jews—their progeny included such figures as Marx, Freud, Einstein, and Wittgenstein as well as Trotsky and Weizmann— and they effectively created a climate in which the Russian Jews could slough off the *shtetl* mentality and begin their tortuous entry into the modern world. The efforts of the *maskilim* to assimilate into Western society while keeping at least part of traditional Judaism continued after 1881 to dominate Jewish life.

The Russian Haskalah had its origins in eighteenth-century and early nineteenth-century Germany and Galicia and drew inspiration from the spirit of liberalism and reform which swept Europe after the

French revolution. The Russian government, for all its antisemitic policies, encouraged and sometimes actively promoted the Haskalah as a solution to the perennial Jewish problem—as a way of 'Russifying' the Jews, assimilating them, and making them useful to Russia. The German Haskalah, whose most illustrious figure was Moses Mendelssohn (1729–86), provided an attractive model for success. In eighteenth-century Germany the Jews had been in a state of backwardness comparable to that of the Russian Jews. Hebrew had proved useful—notably in the German translation of the Pentateuch which Mendelssohn edited—as a catalyst for education and German patriotism among them. Having gained the rudiments of a secular German education, these Jews had begun to play a prominent role in the economic and cultural life of Germany, and the use of Hebrew had declined.

The tsarist government allowed Hebrew to develop as it was seen as a potentially valuable tool of education, reform, and Russian nationalism as well as a means of breaking down the religious and social defences which protected the Jews from assimilation and, ultimately, conversion. A small group of Hebrew writers, notably the essayists Isaac Ber Levinsohn (1788–1860) and Mordecai Aron Guenzberg (1795–1846), and the poet Abraham Dov Lebensohn (1794?–1878), formed the nucleus of the early Russian Haskalah. These were followed by such figures as Abraham Mapu (1808–67), the first Hebrew novelist, and Judah Leib Gordon (1831–92), the most important poet of the Haskalah. In the face of severe opposition, the *maskilim* made valiant efforts to bring about much-needed social and educational reform. Unlike the government, they wished to preserve a large measure of Jewish tradition and social cohesion. Though their use of Hebrew was poor for the most part, they prepared the ground for the flourishing of the language later in the century. Unfortunately, in their writings at any rate, they often accepted the prejudices encouraged by the church and government that the Jews were morally inferior, backward, parasitical, deserving of condemnation, and in need of reform. They shunned the idea of Jewish national consciousness and effectively acted as agents of assimilation. They accepted that education and social change among the Jews were fair pre-conditions to the abolition of the Pale of Settlement and emancipation. Among the Jewish masses, in contrast, the private attitude towards the government, especially during the reign of Nicholas I, was of loathing and disgust.

The Russian Haskalah evolved in three distinct phases, all in Mendele's lifetime, and vividly described in his writings:

1. The reigns of Alexander I (1801–25) and Nicholas I (1825–55), when its impact was negligible.
2. The first part of the reign of Alexander II (1855–81), until the Polish revolt of 1863, when its influence, especially among the young, was considerable.
3. The period of disillusionment and decline in the latter part of the reign of Alexander II (1863–81), leading up to his assassination and the outbreak of the pogroms.

It is hard nowadays to picture the enormous resistance among the Russian Jews to enlightenment and change in any form during the reign of Nicholas I. To some extent, the Jews were probably affected by the longstanding attitude of submissiveness among their gentile neighbours in the Pale, of whom the vast majority were serfs. However, the Jews were at a particular disadvantage at this time because the tsar's backward, oppressive policies towards the Jews ensured that they would turn inward for comfort and protection and cling fervently to their ancient way of life. The more ancient and authoritative the wisdom, the better, according to Benjamin (79); and this, generally, was the principle governing the lives of most Russian Jews at the time. Not only was Russian viewed with suspicion, but even Hebrew works, if not rabbinically approved, were seen as a threat to the Jewish religion, and at times these books were condemned even without being read (72).

The Russian Jews prior to the 1850s were afraid of secular education. They associated it with assimilation and conversion to Christianity. Although Russian schools were legally open to the Jews, and had been since 1804, Christian religious education was compulsory. In 1840, of the total of 80,017 pupils in the Russian primary and secondary schools, only 48 were Jewish![1]

This fear of education was by no means unjustified as Alexander I and Nicholas I alike were in favour of Jewish conversion and used both persuasion and force to induce it. Furthermore, the rabbinic authorities were opposed to secular education as it would increase awareness among the Jews of their legal disabilities and turn them away from Judaism. For these reasons, the passage of a law in 1844 allowing the

---

[1] Greenberg, *The Jews in Russia*, i. 32.

Jews to open their own schools, in which secular subjects would be taught, aroused fear and suspicion rather than celebration.

In *Of Bygone Days*, Mendele gives a vivid semi-comic account of the dismay caused among the Russian Jews by the law of 1844. At this time he was a young boy and the very idea of Haskalah was probably unknown to him. He came home one day to the sound of 'screaming and crying, as if for the dead' (275). Looking back at this incident some sixty years later, the author must have smiled at the irony that he, who had devoted much of his life to the Haskalah, had actually gone on to fast together with his family to protest a law which, in theory at least, made possible the spread of Haskalah. Not until the period of reform of Alexander II did the Russian Jews feel sufficiently confident to send their children to secular schools freely and in relatively large numbers, without fear that they would be subjected to Christian missionary propaganda. Until then, they had lived in almost medieval benightedness.

The barriers to secular education among the Russian Jews meant that even by the end of the nineteenth century, a hundred years after they came under tsarist rule, the majority of them were largely ignorant of Russian. Mendele, for example, did not learn Russian until his late teens or early 20s. Though he apparently learned to read Russian fluently, he never fully mastered spoken Russian. Dubnow recalled that even in old age, Mendele spoke Russian haltingly and with errors.[2] Disdain for Russian (paralleled in the contempt which many Jewish writers—including Yiddish ones—felt toward Yiddish) was, in fact, not uncommon among educated Russians, who thought little of native Russian culture and preferred French as the language of civilization and enlightenment. (Many illustrations of this are found in *War and Peace*, in which the Russian aristocrats often speak to one another in French.) However, the Jews' ignorance of Russian held back their integration into Russian society and increased distrust and revulsion among the ignorant and already prejudiced peasantry among whom they lived. Mendele satirizes this ignorance in *The Travels of Benjamin the Third*, set during the Crimean War. Benjamin, testing his courage by going alone into the forest, is scared out of his wits by a cart-driving peasant. He falls into a dead faint and the peasant carts him home. He comes to on the way and the peasant asks him in Russian if he feels better. 'Benjamin was very confused: he knew no Russian. Even Rashi

[2] Dubnow, 'Zikhronot', 404.

with his medieval French was none too clear to him, and how was he going to reply? How could he find out where he was being taken?' (61). The mutual ignorance and lack of understanding between the Russian Jews and the peasants is satirized further, after Benjamin and Senderel set out on foot, mapless, for the Land of Israel and encounter a peasant.

'Senderel,' said Benjamin, 'since this gentile has come our way, let's ask him directions. We've got nothing to lose. Go, talk to him. Here, outside Eretz Yisrael, you're better at talking to the peasants in their own crude language. Didn't you always tag along after your wife in the market and carry the food home?'

Senderel went over to the peasant. He bowed down and said something like this:

'Good morning! Tell me, mister. Which way to Eretz Yisrael?'

'What?' said the peasant, staring at him, astonished. 'What Srul? I don't know no Srul!'

'Ni! Ni!' Benjamin burst in, unable to contain himself. 'Goy, you don't understand. You say Srul, he say Eretz Yisrael. Senderel, tell him again, this time clear. He's got brains of a donkey. Tell him clear, Senderel!'

'To Erretz Yisrael, which way?' Senderel spat it out.

'The Devil take you, Jews! What are you messing me about for? This road goes to Shikkerville [Drunksville] and they—Elassel! Elassel!' He mocked them, spat in their faces and moved on. (67)

Senderel's Russian, picked up in the market, is comically ineffective elsewhere, too. In one scene, he and Benjamin are in a rowing boat on a lake, practising overseas travel. He tries to question the gentile 'captain' about the ten lost tribes of Israel. 'Senderel suffered greatly during this conversation, as he stammered away, gesticulating hand and foot, sweating from the labour of it. The captain stared darkly at him, spitting and muttering in disgust. Benjamin prodded him on, anxious to hear what the man had to say' (79). In the end, their ignorance of Russian leads Benjamin and Senderel to mistake a recruiting office for a bath-house, with the result that they are drafted unwittingly into the Russian army!

The Jews' ignorance of Russian and of educational works in Hebrew consigned them to backwardness. Mendele mocks the ease with which Benjamin is impressed by the provincial 'accomplishments' of the Batlonites.

I was sure that no one was as clever and wise as Reb Itzig-Dovid ben Reb Aharon-Yossel—they say that in his youth he knew fractions, a branch of wisdom which not every one of us has learned, not even the greatest business-man and shopkeeper. Reb Itzig-Dovid should have been a government minister, but 'Jews have no luck' [Shab. 156a]. I was sure that no one was more articulate or spoke more sweetly than our Chaikel the Stutterer. And who to revive the dead like our doctor, Asya the specialist, who trained, we hear, with an Egyptian gypsy sorcerer! (59)

Chaikel the Stutterer appears later in the story in connection with his theory that a miraculous feather accounts for the operation of all machinery (71). Another belief, probably not uncommon among the Russian Jews in the 1840s, is alluded to in *Of Bygone Days*. A letter from America arrives in a Lithuanian *shtetl*, giving rise to the question, 'How can men go from one side of the earth to our side without falling off?' (300).

Mendele's writings are scattered with superstitions, most of which he had himself witnessed, and in some cases believed, as a child.[3] Often these had carried over from traditional beliefs, for example in transmigration of souls, the idea that an animal might once have been human and vice versa. As a child, Mendele heard a tale of a slaughtered goose which had run away—it had a human soul: 'From then on, Shloyme believed in the transmigration of souls: a goose was no goose, a cat no cat—a man no man, and an animal no animal, but each had changed from another. And our entire world was nothing but a figment of the imagination' (275). Other superstitions described by Mendele include the following: if a pregnant woman removed the teat of an *etrog* (citron) with her teeth, she would have a safe labour (16); if a cow did not give enough milk, witches were to blame (274); a black spot in milk was a demon of malaria (ibid.); the wishes of the dead as expressed in dreams had to be obeyed—otherwise bad luck (the 'Evil Eye') would follow (147); the souls of the dead prayed in synagogue by night (272).

One of Mendele's earliest memories, related in *Of Bygone Days*, was of an exorcist who visited Kopyl when he was about 9 or 10, i.e. around the time when the law of 1844 was passed. His sister-in-law was giving birth and the exorcist fought off a demon which threatened the baby.

On the other side of the furnace a strong light shone from the room, the room used by his brother and sister-in-law. He lay flat, moving forward to see what was going on there. His flesh shuddered in fear at what he saw. His sister-in-law's bed stood behind the curtain. Clusters of needles, sparkling in the candlelight, hung above the curtain from one end to the other. The stool by the

---

[3] On Mendele's own superstitions as a child see p. 35 above.

furnace had disappeared, leaving a hole in the earth like an open grave. A terrifying human form stood holding a black rooster, burning incense, making horrible contortions, beating the rooster's head, whispering in a strange intonation—'Aia-beia, stitaya, agrefti, meirum, shmariel'—rolling his eyes, blowing, whispering—'Matzafatz, metzafatz, matzifatz, matzafatz, metzeifatz, metzefatz, metzafetz, metzifetz'—kicking, pushing with his hand as if struggling with his enemy and, at every word, beating the rooster's head, till it wailed, gabbled, shuddered in pain. Suddenly a scream came from behind the curtains together with a heart-rending sigh. The man convulsed himself all the more, he held his breath and moaned as if the words were coming from his stomach—'Tilmecha, chaishe, uvesusbik, pesalmigya'—gripping the rooster by the neck, waving it round his head as if it were Yom Kippur eve; he strangled it, tossed it into the hole, covered it with earth, and the stool was put back in its place. No sooner had he covered the hole than a powerful cry came from behind the curtain, and a softer cry with it. Shloyme's mother and another woman poked their heads between the drapes and said: '*Mazal tov!* It's a boy! May God grant him long life!' (273)

Prior to the 1840s, there were no trained Russian Jewish doctors. Medicine in the Pale was almost entirely in the hands of the rabbis, quacks, and faith-healers. Their 'methods' included: bleeding with leeches (253), rolling eggs or pouring wax over the patient (317), and medicine made of willow leaves (51). In some cases, they recommended the incantation of biblical or rabbinic sayings inverted into nonsense, or the alteration of the patient's name to cheat death (ibid.). Life expectancy was not much more than 45 (38, 47). Epidemics were not uncommon and their etiology was not known (346); paupers might be hastily married off in the graveyard to frighten the plague away (97). Recovery from illness was, in some places, a qualification to practise medicine: Mendele's father, Reb Chaim, allegedly having once come close to death, was consulted by the critically ill (266). By the same token, Mendele wryly adds, a certain local criminal was thought to be a legal expert as he had spent time behind bars. There were 'specialists' in all areas, each with his own remedies, some possibly efficacious, most founded on superstition.

Superstition was, of course, bound up with religion. A temperate, moral life with regular prayer and the observance of the Sabbath and the *mitzvot* (religious precepts) was believed literally to ward off the devil. The High Holy Days were no mere ritual but a reality, a time of judgment,

when the heavens storm and God sits on his holy throne and angels rush back and forth, saying, 'Behold the Day of Judgment!' Books are opened before

Him, sealed with each man's fate. All humanity troops before Him as He weighs their deeds, numbers them and decides: who will live and who will die, who will be killed by wild beasts and who will die in riots, who will find rest and who will move—by land or by sea, to the four winds. (269)[4]

Terror at the Day of Judgment carried over to the festival of Sukkot (Tabernacles), as seen in the following superstition associated with Hoshanah Rabbah, the seventh day of Sukkot: 'Many sit in synagogue chanting the final verses of the Torah, stealing frightened glances at the wall to see if their shadow was still there—this being a sign that they would live—or if their shadow had vanished—signifying that they would die that year' (11). As for the *maskilim*, who rejected superstition and called for educational and religious reform—hell awaited them! Mendele tells with amused irony of his horror as a child when he first heard of a species of Jew that did not behave exactly like the Jews of Kopyl: 'A Jew—without a hat! A Jew—eating without washing his hands and saying the blessing! Have the Berlin Jews gone out of their minds? Don't they know what's waiting for them in hell? Traps, fire and brimstone, and trails of flame!' (277).[5] The early Russian *maskilim*, it is important to stress, were strictly orthodox Jews, hardly different in appearance or behaviour from other Russian Jews. Yet the suspicion and hatred which they roused often led to their being hounded, physically harassed, and driven from their homes (34–5); as mentioned previously, this happened to Mendele. The *maskilim* are described by Mendele as a courageous minority of idealists who went against the current. He looked back upon these pioneers of social revolution with nostalgia tinged with irony, for they burned with 'the fire of love for all men, brethren all, whether Jews or non-Jews . . . They envisaged a world in the making, a brave new world which they were bringing, expectantly, into being. Soon light would spring from darkness, the earth be transformed to a Garden of Eden, the heavens would approve and give comfort and salvation to mankind' (186).

These *maskilim*, while deeply critical of Jewish life, were driven by constructive goals. They encouraged pride in Jewish tradition and in the Hebrew language, especially of the Bible, 'the eternal language of our people, holding our finest treasures, making us a nation in exile— the people of the Book' (14). To raise national morale in time of

---

[4] This passage echoes the Hebrew meditation beginning *Unetaneh tokef* and recited during the *musaf* (Additional) service on the High Holy Days.

[5] This passage is quoted also on pp. 36–7 above.

degradation, they stressed the Jews' vital role in civilization as 'a great nation, from the start a light to the nations; their Torah teaches life, love of freedom, compassion, peace' (19).

A strength of the Haskalah was that it did not stay aloof but took spiritual and intellectual nourishment from the very groups it set out to change: the *hasidim* and their rivals, the *mitnagdim*. The *maskilim* seem to have combined the fervid optimism of the *hasidim* with the rationalism of the *mitnagdim*. (This was true of Mendele, born in Lithuania, a major centre of the *mitnagdim*, but who spent much of his life in towns with a strong *hasidic* character, such as Berdichev.) However, the chief enemies of the *maskilim* were the *hasidim*, steeped in superstition, clinging tenaciously to their faith in their *rebbe* almost as a God-like figure. These *rebbe*s sometimes abused the trust of their disciples. The portrait of the *hasidic* couple, Ephraim and Sarah, in *Fathers and Sons*, though satirical in tone, still gives an authentic picture of the forces with which the *maskilim* had to contend. It contrasts strikingly with *The Mare*, written a bare five years later.

Ephraim is the antithesis of all that the Haskalah stood for. He is an ignoramus. He judges books by whether they were printed in Vilna, where Haskalah books were published, or in Zhitomir, where the press was controlled by the *hasidim* (23). Barely literate, he knows nothing of Hebrew grammar, which no self-respecting *maskil* could forgive. He sneers at secular books (22–3). A thoroughgoing materialist, he is obsessed with status, money, and social standing. Tyrannical at home, he creates friction with his family, behaving crassly to his wife, engaging his daughter, Rachel, to an odious man whom she despises, and virtually driving his son, Simon, from home. In short, he is little different from the domineering patriarchs often found in Victorian society. The piles from which he has suffered since marriage evidently symbolize (and satirize) the soreness in his family life (31).

As for Sarah, her limited horizons are exposed when she pays a visit to her *rebbe*. Desperate to find Simon—he has run away from home to join the *maskilim* and get an education—the gullible woman is granted an audience with the old charlatan. The scene recalls Turgenev's *Smoke*, in which the self-appointed prophet and intellectual, Gubaryov, is received by his devotees.

'Come in, wife of Ephraim!' said the old man to Sarah when he heard her at the door. 'I know you have suffered bitterly.'

'He's a prophet,' said Sarah to herself. 'I've not told him my problems and already he knows. He's the best Ba'al Shem there is . . .'

'What pain I've suffered!' Sarah cried, hands extended. 'My only son has run away and I am bereaved. What will become of me?' As she spoke, she gave him the slip of paper with her wish as well as the fee.

'Didn't I tell you from the start, twenty years ago, when you asked me for a son, that two ways lay ahead: to remain barren or to bear a son and suffer for it?'

'Woe is me!' cried Sarah, wiping nose with all five fingers. 'Who wants to be barren, to have no *kaddish* . . . And how could I stop myself from accepting your fine gift rather than be childless and unhappy! You said then that my case was not hopeless: if you could grant me a son, could you not change the evil decree and make my son righteous?'

'What has your son done?' asked the *rebbe*, lifting his eyes upward and sighing piously.

'Nothing wrong, far from it!' Sarah replied. 'Just that he's gone astray, to study and become enlightened.'

'Enlightened!' cried the *rebbe*, raising his voice, angry and fearful as if the name of his arch-enemy had been uttered. 'Could there be anything worse?'

'Can nothing be done? Is it beyond help?' Sarah lamented bitterly.

'What did your son study?'

'The Bible,' Sarah replied, voice trembling.

'My God, my God!' sighed the *rebbe*. (30–1)

For all their stupidity, neither Sarah nor Ephraim is entirely un-sympathetic. Ephraim is deeply troubled by his children. He suffers nightmares of guilt over the way he treats his son (26). He sees the error of trying to force his daughter to marry. In the end, too, he is ruined when his business collapses, and he recognizes to his horror that the *rebbe* is a fraud. The *maskil* Ben-David, true to his Haskalah values, helps him. On his death-bed, Ephraim acknowledges the virtues of the Haskalah and approves Ben-David's marriage to his daughter.

Even in its revised form, *Fathers and Sons* is the weakest and most propagandistic of Mendele's novels. It lacks the ideological tension of later works such as *The Mare*, in which the Haskalah is called into question, or *The Beggar Book*, in which the protagonist, Fishke the Lame, is no *maskil* and actually disapproves of the Haskalah. The chief weakness in Mendele's delineation of character in *Fathers and Sons* is that ideological leanings indicate moral stature.[6] The heroes are *maskilim*, the villains *hasidim*. Ben-David, the flawless *maskil*, combines rare qualities of intellect and feeling and does good for its own sake. Worldly as well as idealistic, he bears no grudge against Ephraim and

[6] On this weakness as a general feature of the Hebrew literature of the period, see Patterson, *The Hebrew Novel in Czarist Russia*.

Sarah for treating him cruelly. He is a man in love. The *hasid* Ben-Peretz, in contrast, is totally unsuited to Rachel, yet Ephraim first betrothes her to him. Apart from his flaws in character, his ears are like hairy pancakes and he dribbles when he talks! His only redeeming feature, one feels, is that he eventually becomes a *maskil*.

For all its faults, *Fathers and Sons* was a crucial step forward in Mendele's progress as a Hebrew writer, and it has an important place in the growth of Hebrew literature. It was only the second Hebrew novel set in the contemporary era (the first was Mapu's *The Hypocrite*, 1867). The social issues which preoccupied the *maskilim* are described in greater detail in this novel than in any other by Mendele.

One of these issues was women's rights, then in its infancy in Russia. In *Fathers and Sons*, Rachel bemoans her fate as a woman. She tells her brother:

You're a man and can do what you please. If you want to study—you can choose where. The whole world is open to you. But I'm a woman. A woman's life is confined to her father's house when she's growing up and, later, to her husband's house. What am I? What will become of me? (11)

While Jewish men were, in fact, severely limited in opportunities, the women were at an even greater social disadvantage. They were all too often treated like sheep or cattle (13, 379–80); or married off against their will and used virtually as battery hens (145). In *Fathers and Sons*, Sarah shows no concern whatever for Rachel's happiness. She wants her daughter married to avoid the shame of having an unmarried daughter of 18. When Rachel insists on seeing the groom, Sarah exclaims: 'A Jewish girl—talking back ... like that! Have you ever seen anything like it!' (36). Single Jewish men were also vulnerable to stigma (318 ff.).

As for romantic love, the very idea, Mendele writes, was foreign to the Jews of the Pale. The family was the bastion of Jewish life, a refuge in a hostile world. Divorce was rare. Mendele looked back on the attitude to love which prevailed in his childhood.

'Loveliness is lies, beauty is vanity', Scripture says, and sexual love can never last. Whoever builds his family life and happiness on it builds on sand, trusts in the spider's web. Today a fragrant rose, tomorrow faded. Today I love you—tomorrow, someone else. (279–80)

One of the chief bugbears of the Haskalah, and Mendele in particular, was the treatment of children, who often had no childhood. The practice of child marriage was common among the Russian Jews, though probably no more than among other groups in the Russian empire. Mendele recalled that in Kopyl boys and girls would normally be married by age 13 (280). He himself escaped this fate only by accident. In fact, it was not unusual for children of 8 or 9, or even younger, to be married (281), especially during the reign of Nicholas I, when the communally appointed child snatchers were on the prowl. Ephraim and Sarah in *Fathers and Sons* met for the first time as children on their wedding day, and this was not at all unusual.

Social change was inevitable, but the upheaval caused by the Haskalah had its victims. The adoption of Haskalah ideas or the befriending of a *maskil* not infrequently led to communal division, family disruption, and even family break-up. *In the Valley of Tears* tells of a young married woman who comes under the influence of a *maskil* and then falls in love with him. Unhappy at home, she divorces her husband and marries the *maskil*. In 'No Peace for Jacob', a husband and wife who are devoted to one another and have a young daughter are forced by social pressure to divorce after the husband is accused of Haskalah heresy. A similar tragedy occurred in Mendele's family in the 1840s, he relates in *Of Bygone Days*. His sister, Leah, was happily married, but her husband had friends with Haskalah leanings. His father-in-law, Mendele's father, reacted with bitter recriminations. The marriage collapsed and the couple divorced.

The Haskalah also stimulated harsh self-criticism and self-hate among its adherents, as I have shown in the previous chapter. No creature, writes Mendele, is sadder than a Jew who starts to think (412).

However, the problems created by the Haskalah paled in comparison with those which it set out to solve. The Haskalah viewed mankind optimistically, much as the eighteenth-century French Rationalists had done: the natural world is good and man is born good, but his ignorance has led to his depravity and to the spoilage of nature, through materialism and the rise of industry. Mendele alludes to this idea in *The Mare*, when the Devil condemns mankind: 'when you got hold of this perfect world you ruined it, like a baby who tears a clock to pieces' (334).

The Jews in Mendele's writings exemplify this unnatural, but not irretrievably corrupt, side of humanity. Their character, history, and ritual are often depicted as clashing with nature. In the opening of *The Beggar Book*, the Jews are alien to the natural world and incapable of enjoying it in their present condition. Inhibited by their religion, they are immersed in suffering, past and present. Ironically, the livelihood of Mendele the Bookpeddler—and, in a sense, of his creator—depends on the perpetuation of these sufferings.

No sooner does the warm wind start to blow and summer comes in, and the world of the Holy One, blessed be He, is full of light and joy—than the Jews begin to mourn, fast and weep, from the time of the counting of the Omer[7] until the rainy season. This is the high season for me, Mendele the Bookpeddler, when I travel through the towns in the Pale to sell the Jews the tools of tears—that is, books of lamentations, penitential prayers, rams' horns, holiday prayer books, the Book of Supplication [for women], the Confessional Prayer [for the eve of Yom Kippur], and similar books which set you up for a good cry. The Jews spend the summer in tears and mourning—and I do business. But that's beside the point. (91)

This mockery of Jewish mourning and self-denial could easily have had the Russian peasants for its target: the two groups were not dissimilar in religious fervour, superstition, and occasional mortification of the flesh.[8] To the Jews of the Pale, as to the Russian peasants, nature came second to religion or, at any rate, was absorbed in it. Mendele does not disparage the religious feelings of the Jews, only those customs which he regards as symptoms of collective psychological illness. In an aside in *In the Valley of Tears*, he suggests that while the Jews might not value the nightingale's song, they were elevated spiritually by the cantorial songs of the liturgy (160).

One of the most charming features of Mendele's writings is, in fact, his 'Judaization' of nature, leading to all sorts of strange, whimsical images. Frogs croak—from an appropriate psalm as Benjamin and Senderel set out on their journey (66). Elsewhere, a cow stands like a preacher at his pulpit (67), a raven wears a striped black and white

---

[7] The counting of the omer (lit. 'sheaf of corn'): 49 days between the second day of Passover and Pentecost. This period, with the exception of Lag ba'omer (the 33rd day of the *omer* = 18 Iyar), is a time of mourning in commemoration of the massacres perpetrated by the Romans during the Bar Kochba revolt, 132–5 CE.

[8] 'In contrast with [the feasts celebrated by the peasants] were the severe fasts practised on almost half the days of the year, when the consumption of meat, milk, butter and eggs was forbidden. In each week Wednesday (the day on which Judas betrayed Christ) as well as the more familiar Friday, was a fast day. And there were four more or less prolonged fasts in addition to this: Lent; St Peter's Fast (lasting five weeks and ending on 29th June, the day of St Peter and St Paul); the Fast of the Assumption (two weeks before 15th August); and the Christmas Fast (six weeks ending on 24th December).' Ronald Hingley, *Russian Writers and Society, 1825–1904* (New York, 1967), 124–5.

prayer shawl and prays (93), storks are like women at the ritual bath dipping modestly into the water (101), a horse and a team of oxen naturally say grace after meals (105), another horse is compared to a recalcitrant *cheder* pupil (133), the green hill near Kesalon is likened to the Mount of Olives and the Lebanon (140).

Nevertheless, the Jews in Mendele's world have little appreciation of nature, and less understanding of it. Ignorance of and alienation from the natural world among the Jews was one of Mendele's chief worries as a *maskil*. His most ambitious work, *Natural History*, aimed to help the Jews overcome their ignorance of this subject. In fact, *Natural History* had relatively little impact, except among the *maskilim*, who were a tiny percentage of the Russian Jews; its main importance in retrospect was that by writing it Mendele developed a brilliant descriptive style. His clear, detailed accounts of the natural world in his fiction would have been almost inconceivable without this self-imposed training. However, *Natural History* does show how far Mendele had himself come since childhood. For in one of the key passages in *Of Bygone Days*, he admits how little he had known of the world around him. His imagination then was rooted, fascinatedly, in the Bible and Talmud. He had fixed in his mind a whole array of animal, vegetable, and mineral species which he had never seen—the only zoo he saw as a child was the human one around him—and some of which had never existed.

Of the natural world, with its variety of plants, animals and birds, Shloyme knew nothing. What did he care for the rye, the buck-wheat and potatoes, his daily fare? The harvest in the fields surrounding his village, the nearby forest and its trees, meant nothing to him. His imagination was full of other things: mandrakes, myrrh, onycha, galbanum, vines, dates, figs, pomegranates, olives, acacia-wood and gopher-wood. Of animal species he knew: the he-goat from the time of Moses; the lion and leopard who taught might and valour to the Children of Israel; the hind, which taught them to run, like himself, in urgent haste; the wild ox crouching over a thousand hills; the buffalo which was so big—like Mount Tabor—that only its nose could fit into Noah's ark. Of creeping things he knew the viper and the *shamir*, created on Sabbath-eve at twilight and used to cut stone for the Temple in Jerusalem; and he knew of nits. Of birds he knew the turtle-dove, the wild cock which had brought the *shamir*, the *bar-yochna*, an egg of which had once fallen and drowned sixty cities and broken three hundred cedar trees; and the *ziz-sadai*, that great bird whose wings block the sunlight. In short, Shloyme may have been born in the village, but he lived elsewhere . . . in time past, in a world that was no longer. He lived temporarily in this world, but his permanent residence was in that world. He visited his parents' house briefly, like a guest at an inn. He would eat and sleep and the next day would return to the other world . . . His way of life was that of thousands of other Shloymeles—in memoriam, in memory of an ancestral way of life. As their ancestors had done, so did they, to fulfil what is written and even what is not written: That is the way they lived in those days. (272)[9]

As a *maskil* who regarded the love of nature as one of the more attractive 'conditions' for enlightenment, and who spent more years on *Natural History* than on any of his novels, Mendele filled his works with paeans to the beauty of the natural world which rank with the finest in Hebrew. Eventually, he indicates in *The Mare*, he came to regard this condition with ambivalence, as yet another of the 'toys' or 'tricks', the mastery of which would bring the Jews no closer to emancipation.

The early part of Mendele's career coincided with the 'golden age' of the Haskalah, from 1855 to 1863, when such reforms as the abolition of juvenile conscription and the admission of wealthy and professionally trained Jews into the Russian interior—as well as the optimistic spirit of the period—gave rise to the hope that emancipation was not long in coming. In fact, the reforms were reluctant concessions by Tsar Alexander II to increasing demands, during and after the Crimean War, for social and political change. They reflected his fear that adamant resistance to the current of the times might lead to the disruption of his empire. The Jews were unaware of the tsar's motives; they, and the *maskilim* in particular, saw the tsar as their benefactor. Pathetically eager at this time to bridge the gap separating them from the Russians, they 'interpreted a friendly gesture on the part of non-Jews as evidence of a complete change of heart'.[10]

Prior to 1881, many of the *maskilim*—dazzled by Western culture, ashamed of Jewish backwardness, overwhelmed by government power—fell in with the official view that emancipation was not an inalienable right, but that the Jews had to earn it by educating and 'Russifying' themselves—'prancing round a ring, leaping through a

---

[9] A comparable sense of detachment from nature is expressed by Isaac Babel in the story 'Awakening' (1930). The autobiographical narrator, raised by his family to be a violin prodigy but keen to be a writer, is attached to the powerfully built, aged Jew, Yefim Nikitich Smolich, who tries to induce in him a love of nature: ' "What's that tree?" I didn't know. "What's growing on that bush?" I didn't know this either. "What bird is that singing?" I knew none of the answers . . . "And you dare to write! A man who doesn't live in nature, as a stone does or an animal, will never in all his life write two worthwhile lines" '; *Collected Stories*, tr. W. Morison, Penguin edn. (Harmondsworth, Middx., 1974), 272–3.

[10] Greenberg, *The Jews in Russia*, i. 84.

hoop', as the Devil puts it in *The Mare*—and by making themselves useful to the empire. The *maskilim* of course wanted the spread of secular education for its own sake. But in so far as they promoted the idea that emancipation depended on education—at root a form of cultural blackmail—they betrayed the inferiority and shame which they felt as Jews. In common with Russian liberal thinkers, their all-absorbing obsession with education and emancipation blinded them to the dire economic realities of the Pale. The reforms of Alexander II led neither to emancipation nor to any substantial betterment of the conditions of the Jews. On the contrary, the tsar clearly had no intention of abolishing the Pale, and the economic plight of the Russian Jews worsened. University-trained Jews struggling for a useful, dignified place in Russian society found that they were hated as fiercely as their brothers in the Pale. The Haskalah had made no difference. In Odessa in 1871 the first major pogrom took place with tacit government approval. From then on, the Jews were periodically used as scapegoats to divert revolutionary violence away from the government, and subjected to further legislative discrimination and economic restrictions that caused immense upheaval and hardship. According to a Russian government report of the 1880s, 90 per cent of the Jews constituted 'a proletariat living from hand to mouth, in poverty and under the most trying and unhygienic conditions'.[11] By 1900, approximately 40 per cent of the Russian Jews were living permanently or periodically on charity.[12]

Against this background of economic privation and gathering anti-semitism, the educational ideals of the Haskalah seemed trivial. As Leon Pinsker wrote in 'Autoemancipation' during the pogroms, the Jews were wrong to assume that the forces governing them were necessarily good. 'Instead of realizing their own position and adopting a rational line of conduct, the Jews appeal to eternal justice, and fondly imagine that the appeal will have some effect.'[13] The failure of this appeal, which is forcefully satirized in *The Mare*, was the death-blow to the Haskalah movement.

Disillusionment with Enlightenment ideals was felt also by Russian intellectuals. The Devil's attack on the Haskalah echoes Turgenev's *Fathers and Sons*, where Bazarov dismisses so-called reforms in the

---

[11] Greenberg, *The Jews in Russia*, i. 160.
[12] James Parkes, *A History of the Jewish People*, Pelican edn. (London 1964), 166.
[13] Leon Pinsker, 'Autoemancipation', in Robert Chazan and M. I. Raphael (eds.), *Modern Jewish History: A Source Book* (New York, 1974), 167.

face of the relentless poverty in Russia. Mendele's mare is ill-bred and unschooled, dirty and repugnant, and she grazes in the pastures of others; and for this reason the Society for the Prevention of Cruelty to Animals refuses to help her unless she becomes 'educated'. The Devil gives four reasons why the Haskalah for her is futile and ludicrous.

You tell this miserable creature: 'Get an education!' I'm asking you: First, why pick on her? There are plenty of unschooled animals, even lowly horses and donkies, who provide for themselves unhindered. If only the mare were as fat as they! Second, it's true that she was never stable-trained. Stallion tricks mean nothing to her. Still, she's not totally ignorant like a common horse or donkey. Third, though she has none of the entertainment value of the trained horses, she's more useful: they hunt and pull chariots but she's worn down by hard work. Yes, whatever people may say, she serves a function and her work has permanent value. Fourth, what does livelihood have to do with Haskalah? Who has the right to make education a prior condition to eating and breathing? God made every creature with senses and limbs for the especial purpose of staying alive. A mouth—to eat; a nose—to breathe; legs—to walk; and everything else is like circus tricks—prancing round a ring, leaping through a hoop—superfluous amusement, things which come last—that's Haskalah. (332)

Translated: the Jews might have been uncouth and backward but, unlike the majority of the Russians (the 'lowly horses and donkies'), they possessed an ancient tradition of religious education and were not totally ignorant. Also, the Jews belonged almost entirely to the working class and contributed greatly to the Russian economy, as government studies showed.[14] In contrast, the Russian aristocrats, who included the 'trained horses', did little or no useful work. But the most important point implied by the Devil is that the Russian government had no right to demand the enlightenment of the Jews as a precondition to granting them, through emancipation, the means of physical survival.

Bazarov, in a similar vein, insists that Russia has her priorities wrong.

Not so very long ago we were saying that our officials took bribes, that we had no roads, no trade, no impartial courts of justice . . . Then we realized that just to keep on and on talking about our social diseases was a waste of time, and merely led to a trivial doctrinaire attitude. We saw that our clever men, our so-called progressives and reformers, never accomplished anything, that we were

[14] Greenberg, *The Jews in Russia*, i. 168–70; I. M. Dijur, 'Jews in the Russian Economy', in J. Frumkin *et al.* (eds.), *Russian Jewry (1860–1917)* (New York, 1966), 120–43.

concerning ourselves with a lot of nonsense, discussing art, unconscious creative work, parliamentarianism, the bar, and the devil knows what, while all the time the real question was getting daily bread to eat.[15]

Levin does, too, in Tolstoy's *Anna Karenina*: 'why schools should cure the ills of poverty and ignorance is as incomprehensible as the idea that hens on their perches cause convulsions. You must first remedy the cause of their poverty.'[16]

This reasoning may be applied to the characters in Mendele's stories. Could one insist that Reb Leib, gruesomely described in 'Earthquake Days', should get an education prior to the improvement of his diet and living conditions?

His body was like a broken earthenware jar or a dry tree, without an ounce of flesh. His hands were shrivelled reeds. His veins were crimson and bloated. His face was a ruin. Sagging cheeks, sunken eyes, a hooked nose like a chimney ravaged by fire, a squashed sparse broom for a beard . . . his dry bones seemed to say to the world: 'Look what befell me!' Each cough was a lament and a cry for his whole bitter life. His life had been nothing more than a long process of dying. (411–12)

Could one fairly ask the typical inhabitant of the Pale to espouse the Haskalah when his poverty took up all his time? In *The Travels of Benjamin the Third*, Mendele paints a comically absurd picture of a pious *luftmentsch* floundering about, trying to persuade himself that he is making a living—and quoting from the Book of Lamentations to prove it! In replying to the question how he makes a living, he says:

May God's name be praised. As sure as I'm standing before you, for example, I've been gifted by the One of blessed name. I can sing. I have a good voice. I serve as a cantor during the High Holy Days in one of the local villages. I'm an expert circumciser and matzo piercer—nobody better. I'm also a matchmaker. I have something that will always be mine—as I'm standing here, for example—a seat in synagogue. By the way—don't let it get out—I have a little whisky at home for sale, and a goat that gives plenty of milk—may the Evil Eye not look upon her—and a wealthy relative nearby who can also be milked if need be. Apart from which, I'm telling you, for example, the Creator, blessed be He, is the merciful Father and the Jews are merciful sons of the merciful, I'm telling you, for example, why should a living man complain [Lam. 3: 39]. (58)

[15] Ivan Turgenev, *Fathers and Sons* [1861], tr. R. Edmonds, Penguin edn. (Harmondsworth, Middx., 1965), 126.
[16] Leo Tolstoy, *Anna Karenina* [1874–6], tr. R. Edmonds, Penguin edn. (Harmondsworth, Middx., 1968), 362.

The insistence upon education as a condition for emancipation was all the more pig-headed and cruel in view of the general backwardness prevailing in Russia. For indeed, we have seen, in comparison with the vast majority of Russians, the Jews were educated. Dostoyevsky in *The House of the Dead* (1860) expresses amazement over the number of literate prisoners among whom he was incarcerated for four years in Omsk, Siberia, in the early 1850s. 'In what other place where ordinary Russians are gathered together in large numbers would you be able to find a group of two hundred and fifty men, half of whom could read and write?'[17] In contrast, most Jewish males, no matter how poor, valued learning and received at least a smattering of religious education: they could read the prayerbook and the Five Books of Moses in Hebrew—without going to Siberia! For this reason, the *maskilim* were able to use Hebrew as a tool for secular education. In *Of Bygone Days*, Mendele recalls the veneration for learning in Kopyl, which generally held true in the Pale. He writes that scholarship was more highly esteemed than wealth. 'No one could gain honour except through being a scholar and God-fearing' (264). In Kopyl, practically all the men studied:

They would gather in the House of Study between the afternoon and evening prayers, to sit or stand round the tables and listen to the preachers expound the Torah, whether the Pentateuch or *aggadah* or *Ein Ya'akov*[18] or ethical wisdom; and on the Sabbath and holidays before the afternoon prayers the preacher would stand wrapped in his prayer shawl on the pulpit by the Holy Ark and preach in style, spicing his words with analogies and proverbs, quotations from the prophets, rabbinic tales and witticisms, kindling in the congregation the fire of holy love for the *Shekhinah*.[19]

The respect which the Russian Jews gave learning was expressed also in the proliferation of *yeshivot*, where no tuition fee was required. Mendele, himself a yeshivah student in the 1840s, describes how the students were supported.

They came not by horse and cart but on foot, penniless. No sooner did they put their pack down—two worn, patched shirts, one pair of socks with dirty,

---

[17] Fyodor Dostoyevsky, *The House of the Dead* [1860], tr. David McDuff, Penguin edn. (Harmondsworth, Middx., 1985), 31.
[18] *Ein Ya'akov*: a collection of legends and homilies from the Talmud, by Rabbi Ya'akov ben Shlomo ibn Haviv, 16th–17th cents.
[19] The *shekhinah*, according to Jewish legend, is the feminine presence of God wandering with the Jews through the Diaspora. See Gershom Scholem, *Major Trends in Jewish Mysticism* (New York, 1974), 229–33.

much-trodden heels—than they came under the town's care. The townspeople, poor as they were, supported these boys willingly. The poorest man in
town shared his bread with a pious scholar—all for the honour of the Torah!
(300)

This learning, however, entailed severe limitations, as Mendele recalls, again in *Of Bygone Days*. In common with most Russian-Jewish
children growing up in the 1840s, his life was circumscribed by the
Talmud—indeed, he knew no other life. A Jew was one who studied
the Torah as expounded in the Talmud. Those who did not study the
Talmud hardly counted.

He was convinced that the Jews had nothing in their world but Talmud, for
study and argument and the reconciliation of the opinions of the rabbis and
commentaries. Jews by definition—so he believed—sharpen one another's
brains with study of the Law. One asks the other: what tractate are you
studying, and how many pages have you learned? Eventually, Shloyme saw that
he had been mistaken. Formerly, he was astonished that some Jews did not
learn Torah—they seemed to be superfluous. Now he became more tolerant:
'Teh! The Holy One, blessed be He, must have wanted these Jews too in His
world!' (278)

Religious study at least helped to preserve Jewish unity and morale.
Secular education had little value in conditions such as those of the
Russian Jews. These conditions are described realistically by Mendele.
The majority of the Russian Jews—in common with the vast majority
of those who lived under tsarist rule—survived on a meagre, irregular
diet, whose staple was often bread or potatoes.[20] Mendele frequently
writes about hunger in the Pale. In his autobiography he recalls that his
daily fare in childhood was rye, buckwheat, and potatoes (272)—and
his family was comparatively well-off. His deepest feelings are for the
children, ground down by hunger and anxiety to a state not unlike that
of the geriatric. Hirshl, in *In the Valley of Tears*, is a typical child of the
Pale who would be perfectly happy if not for the daily gnawing hunger.

There were days when he would come home hungry and worn out from hard
work and wandering through town, but there wasn't a scrap of food in the
house. He had nothing to ease his hunger-pangs. There were times when he
would cry and scratch at himself and tear his fingers through his hair,
screaming, and roll on the floor till he fainted into an exhausted sleep. (152)

Elsewhere, in a bitter comic flight of fancy, Mendele envisages a

[20] Greenberg, *The Jews in Russia*, i. 160–1.

consequence of unremitting hunger—the evolution of a species of Jew with no stomach.

These days there are many Jews with stomachs no bigger than an olive. I'm sure that in future—God willing, and if the meat-tax and the do-gooders don't disappear—the Jews will cut down on food to the point where a generation will evolve without stomachs. Then the Jews will live like angels on this earth. (94)

The Jewish population in the Pale rose from about one million to five million in the course of the nineteenth century. Owing to residence restrictions, most of them eventually became urban residents; and it is estimated that although by the end of the century the Jews comprised 36.9 per cent of the urban population of the Pale, 72.8 per cent of all those engaged in commerce were Jews.[21] As noted in Chapter 1 in the discussion of *In the Valley of Tears*, Mendele pokes sad fun at the population increase among the Jews, their poverty, and the concomitant spread of antisemitism. The Jews of Kabtziel, he writes, may have no distinction other than that of being fruitful and multiplying, an 'accomplishment' which even the most rabid antisemite cannot dispute. Several families frequently lived in one small house, three or four to a room (166). The houses were sometimes little more than 'caves' (77) or 'holes' (377), reminiscent of prehistoric dwellings, and were usually rated 'dangerous for occupation'.[22] Mendele's 'The Fire-Victims' tells of an entire town wiped out by fire, a disaster not uncommon in Russian towns (Bazarov in *Fathers and Sons* points out that these towns burned down every five years[23]).

Disease and epidemics were frequent. In *The Beggar Book*, Mendele writes that the absence of plague in any given year was nothing short of miraculous:

That year there was no plague in Kesalon . . . not that the river and streets were cleaned or that the householders prohibited the throwing of slops into the streets . . . it was a plain miracle. Actually, many Jews caught dysentery and died, but that wasn't the fault of plague. There was another reason—bad cucumbers. (98)

Poor hygiene was to blame for high infant mortality. Mendele gives memorably unsavoury accounts of the filth in Kesalon, of the garbage

[21] Mendes-Flohr and Reinharz (eds.), *The Jew in the Modern World*, 307; *Encyclopaedia Judaica*, 'Pale of Settlement', 13: 27.

[22] Greenberg, *The Jews in Russia*, i. 162.

[23] Turgenev, *Fathers and Sons*, 140. A graphic account of such a conflagration is given by Saltykov-Shchedrin in *The History of a Town: Or the Chronicle of Foolov (1869–70)*, tr. S. Brownsberger (Ann Arbor, 1982).

dumped into the streets among carcasses of cats and dogs, of pigs sinking in mud to their ears (377). In *The Travels of Benjamin the Third*, Mendele describes in detail the sewage 'system' of Kesalon, which held true of Russian towns generally prior to the twentieth century: it consisted of thirty or forty swamps linked through underground channels with the river.

Amid daily hardship and uncertainty, the Jews, like the peasants surrounding them, clung to their religion. One of their few consolations, Mendele writes, was that their society, tottering on the brink of collapse, fulfilled the conditions for the coming of the Messiah (Mish. Sot. 9: 15). 'The Messiah will come speedily in our days. We have no work. Insolence is everywhere. Boys are arrogant to their elders. The vile abuse the honourable. Government restrictions increase daily. The war of Gog and Magog comes near' (145).

With the coming of the Messiah, there would be no more hunger. But who in the meantime would provide for the Jews? The answer is given in *In the Valley of Tears*: a magic ring which in town mythology was granted by Elijah the prophet to a long-dead inhabitant. The owner of this ring would have the power to make all his wishes come true. Unfortunately, the ring has vanished, no one knows where (146–7). The desperation of the Jews, their willingness to clutch at straws, is exemplified in Mendele's account of their emergence from their battered houses on hot summer nights, to engage in hypothetical barter with their Maker:

'Look how many stars there are, milk-white in their orbits! My God, if only He gave me as many gold coins!'

'Fool! I would give Him a better rate, a star for every silver coin . . .'

Then they all chimed in, lowering the rate over and over—two, five, ten stars for a copper coin. (158)

Like these stars, the Jews were themselves devalued as the century went on. But although they were in the gutter, Mendele implies, some of them were looking at the stars.

This, then, was the world of grinding poverty and superstition into which Mendele was born, in which he lived much of his life, and which he passionately loved and despised. His entire career as a writer and educator was taken up with the fight against backwardness and the struggle to enlighten and reform the Jews. The next chapter tells of his own inner struggles and transformation after his father's death.

5
Loss and Wandering in Mendele

THE central, formative trauma of Mendele's early life is unmistakably at the heart of his fiction: the death of his father when he was 13 or 14.[1] This loss caused the break-up of his family, a drastic fall in social status, and economic hardship. It led to his protracted wandering in the Pale of Settlement, culminating in his disastrous first marriage. The emotional turmoil and the conditions caused by the father's death stimulated his earliest creative work and, probably to a large extent, motivated his efforts to satirize and reform Jewish life.

Consequences of his father's death are depicted most vividly in *Of Bygone Days*. Yet virtually all Mendele's major works are preoccupied, in some form or another, with loss or family disruption. The loss of fathers is a recurrent theme: Isaac-Abraham in *The Parasite*, Israel in *The Mare*, Hirshl in *In the Valley of Tears*, the little boy in 'The Calf', Mendele the Bookpeddler himself as seen in 'Warsaw 1881'—have all lost their fathers prematurely. In addition, a number of Mendele's characters are separated from their families and embark on prolonged travels, as Mendele did after his father's death: notably Benjamin and Senderel in *The Travels of Benjamin the Third* and the characters in *The Beggar Book*, including the itinerant Mendele. The ensuing family tragedies which Mendele suffered are shared among his characters: in *Fathers and Sons*, Ben-Aryeh's wife goes mad and he loses his children (similar afflictions occur also in *The Parasite*); and Alter divorces his wife in *The Beggar Book*, a vital piece of background information.

Salient characteristics of Mendele and his work—his humanitarian concern for suffering creatures, especially children, his savage hatred of authority, and his fascination with adolescence and the passage to maturity—derive their intensity from his experience of loss and family break-up. Much of the bitterness and sarcasm in Mendele might be ascribed not only to the hideous social conditions of his age but also

[1] On loss as a precipitant of art, see David Aberbach, *Surviving Trauma: Loss, Literature, and Psychoanalysis* (New Haven, Conn., 1989). Similarly, on the effects of orphanhood on the life and work of Mendele's younger contemporary and disciple, Chaim Nachman Bialik, see David Aberbach, *Bialik* (London, 1988).

to the fact that from his father's death until his divorce he suffered blow after blow, becoming virtually a modern Job.

Over fifty years later, Mendele recalled the shattering effect his father's death had on him. 'With his father's death the world died— the sky turned dark, the woods lost their majesty. Nothing could revive him and restore his former joy in life. The world seemed nothing but a soulless body' (293).[2]

His mother, Sarah-Gnessa, was left with a number of children and few resources. Soon after the burial, she sent him to the nearby town of Timkovichi to ease her financial burden. Here he spent several months, apparently supported by relatives. Prior to his father's death, he relates in *Of Bygone Days*, he was gradually moving away from the fantasy world of his childhood. Now, overcome by grief, he became withdrawn and apathetic. Much of his time was spent in the house of study in a state of deep depression and oblivion.

The Talmud was open in front of him. He rocked back and forth, singing the words softly, sadly. When he got tired he would stiffen like a pole, staring in silence, motionless, into space. Or he would wander into the empty alley of the synagogue to stand and stare at nothing. A fly might land on his nose but he wouldn't notice. A duck might lead its brood into the alley, elongate and lower its head, quack its praise of thanks to the glory of God—he wouldn't see. Cows and goats raising a cloud of dust as they came back from the fields, a young bellowing bull rushing from one cow to the other—he'd be deaf to it all. Finally the beadle would come and tug him from behind: 'Come inside boy, why stand here? It's time for afternoon prayers'. (293)

His father's death scarred Mendele's creative life. In Timkovichi he brooded on his past in Kopyl: his family and home, the persons he had known, the market, the festivals 'rose like the dead from their graves' (294). The need to 'resurrect' or preserve his life prior to his loss might prefigure Mendele's art—his recreation in all its details of *shtetl* life. Indeed, the claim was made prior to the Holocaust that if the *shtetl* world were wiped out, it could be reconstructed using Mendele's writings.[3]

Homesickness drove him home, and this, like all homecomings in

---

[2] Shloyme's alienation from nature as a result of his father's death is strikingly similar to Mendele's response in 'Earthquake Days' (406) to the pogroms; see p. 43 above and p. 112 below.

[3] David Frischmann, 'Mendele Mocher Sefarim', Introd. to *Kol kitvei Mendele*, 3 vol. edn., 1909–12, vol. ii (Odessa, 1911), p. vii. A similar claim was made by James Joyce: if Dublin disappeared, it could be reconstructed through *Ulysses*; see Richard Ellmann, *Four Dubliners* (London, 1987), 56.

Mendele's writings—David's in 'Limdu heitev' (Learn to Do Well, 1862), Hirshl's in *In the Valley of Tears*, Mendele's in 'Warsaw 1881'—was lonely and bitter, reviving memories of the security and comfort he had known and lost. Proud by nature, Mendele felt disgraced by the fall in status and by the unbearable kindness and pity of his friends. He reacted by adopting, even more than previously, an air of superiority, and by becoming fastidious over his honour. He took to wandering in the fields where, he relates in a majestic passage reminiscent of Bialik's poem 'Habereikhah' (The Pool, 1905), his love for nature became a passion and its bittersweet beauty, its God-given sadness and consolation, moulded his creative spirit (297).

Unable to stay with his poor mother and sick of Kopyl, he left soon after for the yeshivah of Slutsk, where he spent two years. He gives a brief, fascinating glimpse of the rat-race and the empty *pilpul* there, the materialism and the obsession with food, and also of his initial problems in making friends and his close friendships later. Yeshivah life, he writes, swallowed him like a swamp, and he lost all desire to study there. He left Slutsk and spent the next couple of years wandering through Lithuania, studying in various other *yeshivot* and houses of study. As he no longer had a secure home, he had little choice, though another motive for these travels might have been the fear of conscription in the Russian army. Several months were also spent in Vilna where, supported by a rich relative, Mendele studied much Talmud and mastered the subject.

Meanwhile, his mother married a miller in the village of Melnick, not far from Kopyl. As we have seen, the first chapter of *Of Bygone Days* is set in Melnick after Mendele, aged 17, tried to join his mother in her new family life, with step-father and his children. He recalled his side of the family steeped in gloom. The miller, an unlearned villager, was a bitter disappointment as a substitute for the erudite, influential Reb Chaim, but Mendele's mother had little choice but to marry him. 'In poverty I had nothing left but to starve. And what would become of the children?' (262).

Mendele disapproved of his mother's remarriage, a crushing reminder of his family's loss of status. He came under severe pressure either to return to yeshivah life, which, he writes, had driven him ragged, or to marry. The awful state of being no longer a youth but not yet a man is conveyed in *The Mare*, in which Israel's widowed mother—she does not remarry—is anxious to see him married, and family and social pressures lead him to breakdown.

Though unhappy at home, Mendele had no wish to marry at this time or to return to the *yeshivot*. His step-father put him to work teaching his untutored children, but he spent much time again wandering alone, reading and dreaming, in the fields and woods near Melnick. In this state of isolation and depression, Mendele began to write: in Hebrew, mostly poetry but also a satiric drama in imitation of the eighteenth-century Italian Hebrew poet and playwright, Moshe Hayyim Luzzatto. Two of the main elements of these works anticipate his mature writings: his love and praise of nature and his tendency to mock human beings, stripping them of pretension. The satanic 'angel of mockery' which incited him to satire, he reveals in his 'Autobiographical Notes' (3), would later rule him in the person of Mendele the Bookpeddler. It is interesting that Gogol too began to write after the death of his father[4] and that other satirists, such as Jaroslav Hašek and P. G. Wodehouse, also lost their fathers early on.

Soon after, apparently in the spring and summer of 1852, there was a momentous and fascinating interlude in Mendele's life: his wanderings, virtually as a beggar, with Abraham the Lame, an itinerant of no fixed profession, who came from Kopyl. Mendele left no direct account of this experience, though *The Travels of Benjamin the Third* and *The Beggar Book* are based partly on it. The story is told by J. L. Binstock (1884) in Russian and by J. H. Ravnitzky (1910) in Hebrew,[5] and as both were in frequent contact with Mendele there would have been much opportunity to make corrections, either orally or in writing, if the details had been wrong. Briefly, Mendele had an uncle who abandoned his family and disappeared. The uncle was spotted in Volhynia by Abraham the Lame who offered to take Mendele's aunt and cousin to Volhynia to find the missing man. With his stories of the good life in Volhynia—the praise of Volhynia is sung also in 'No Peace for Jacob' (392–3)—he persuaded Mendele to come too. (Mendele's mother and step-father were presumably glad to have him off their hands.) This motley band of four set out with battered horse and wagon, wandering from town to town, begging for alms and food. Abraham the Lame, it soon turned out, did not intend to go straight to

---

[4] Henri Troyat, *Gogol: The Biography of a Divided Soul* (London, 1974), 21 ff.

[5] Judah Leib Binstock, 'Letoledotav shel Mendele' (Mendele's Life), tr. from the Russian by Y. Sofer (Joseph Klausner), *Hashiloach*, 34/1 (1918), 14–29 (originally published in *Voskhod* (1884), no. 12); Joshua Hana Ravnitzky, 'Shalom Ya'akov Abramowitz', in *Kol kitvei Mendele* (Collected Works of Mendele Mocher Sefarim), 1922 edn., IV. vii. 24–7.

Volhynia. It suited him to travel about and use the pathetic woman and child and the abject, skinny scholar to beg. He actually concocted a plan to marry Mendele into a wealthy family and to collect a hefty matchmaker's salary. Tension between Mendele and the beggar flared up when he refused to be married off (again!), and the beggar threatened to abandon him. A lucky meeting with a relative allowed Mendele to escape and brought him to Kamenets-Podolsk in time for the High Holy Days.

This story is as good as anything in Mendele's fiction, and one would wish to have a fuller picture of the characters and events, to explore Mendele's methods in transforming autobiography into art. One thing is clear: this journey with its aimless travels and fond hope of a better life would have been inconceivable if Mendele's father had lived. The wanderings, with their constant motion and distraction, appealed to Mendele in his grief. The experience of a bare few months had an enormous impact on Mendele and, later, on his art. He knew from his previous travels how the poor lived—now he was a beggar himself, ragged, unwashed, underfed, sleeping on a bench in the house of study or in the poorhouse, surviving on handouts. In his 'Auto-biographical Notes' (3), as mentioned before, Mendele writes of these events as preordained, a necessary trial readying him for his life as an artist and his archetypal persona as a 'Jew of Jews'. Among the poor he briefly found a lifestyle to suit his wretched state of depression, anxiety, and loss of self-esteem, largely caused by his father's death.

In Kamenets-Podolsk, however, his life changed dramatically. Here he found the direction and purpose which he had sorely lacked. Soon after his arrival, he was recognized by prominent townsmen as a brilliant talmudist and given work as a private tutor. (No wonder he wrote so glowingly later of the reverence for learning among the Jews!) This might have been expected, given his training and sharp intelligence. But the better life which he had hoped to find in Volhynia now drew him to Haskalah. He secretly made the acquaintance of the well-known *maskil* Abraham Ber Gottlober who, together with his daughter Rosalita, taught him secular subjects, including German and Russian.

Again, the loss of his father might underlie Mendele's openness to and need for Haskalah. Especially in view of the immense social pressure on the *maskilim* prior to the reign of Alexander II, it is highly unlikely that he would have chosen to be a *maskil* unless he had felt that the orthodox Jewish world represented by his father, a fanatical enemy of Haskalah, had failed him. By becoming a *maskil*, Mendele expressed both his disillusionment with traditional authority and his need for a benevolent, progressive father-figure such as Gottlober. The reader has only to compare Mendele's father in *Of Bygone Days* with Gutman, the wise, kind *maskil* based on Gottlober in *The Parasite*, to comprehend Mendele's initial attraction to Haskalah. Gottlober, himself part of an isolated, hated minority of *maskilim*, was a true friend to a boy desperate for friendship.

Though he had found his intellectual direction, Mendele now endured a long, devasting tragedy which, like his wanderings, haunted his art. No sooner was he settled in Kamenets-Podolsk than he again came under pressure to marry. The allure of marriage into a wealthy family, which would free him from financial worry for the first time since his father's death and give him good conditions for study, proved too great for him to resist. In 1853 he married. On the surface, his life was ideal: his wife's family was extremely fond of him and his father-in-law was learned and well-to-do, with a large private library. Mendele lived comfortably with his in-laws and prepared for examinations as a government teacher.

Details of the marriage are sketchy but what is known is very sad: Mendele's wife suffered from a mental illness or deficiency, and moreover she bore him two children who died. It may be that she became deranged partly as a result of these losses. According to one testimony,[6] she would sit for hours staring out of the window, suddenly breaking out with strange, heart-rending songs. Married life became increasingly a torture for Mendele, and in 1856 he divorced. He appears to have had lifelong guilt and grief toward both his wife and his lost children. In 'The Memory Book', written nearly sixty years after the divorce, the pleading eyes of a horse recall to the anguished narrator the death of his child (368–9). The bitter memories of Isaac-Abraham in *The Parasite* and Ben-Arye in *Fathers and Sons* of the deaths of their sons and of their wives' mad behaviour apparently have their basis in Mendele's own tragedy. It is interesting, too, that Mendele the Bookpeddler's account of Fishke's bizarre failure of a marriage in *The Beggar Book* is, as the Israeli critic Dan Miron puts it, virtually the only time when he 'lets himself go' and talks to other characters at length and with zest.[7] Guilt over divorce emerges as a central theme in *The Beggar Book*, though the treatment of it is spiced with humour,

---

[6] Related by Klausner in *Historia shel hasifrut ha'ivrit hachadashah*, vi. 334

[7] Miron, *A Traveler Disguised*, 175.

especially in the opening scenes in which Mendele, with comic obnoxiousness, prods Reb Alter to reveal the details of his divorce.

In summary: much of the raw sensitivity and bitterness in Mendele's writings may be traced to the formative period of his adolescence to early manhood (*c.* 1848–56), a period marked by three major tragedies: his father's death, his marriage and divorce, and the loss of two children. These are among the 'unhealed wounds' to which he refers in *Of Bygone Days* (258). During this period, which was interspersed with depression, wanderings, loneliness, and hardship, Mendele gained much of the life experience which later entered his fiction. At this time, too, he began to write, and he also started the long process of self-education by which he eventually perfected his art. The pain of this period was by no means unmitigated by brighter, more hopeful moments and friendships. Yet, on Mendele's own admission, it was hard to bear with only limited support, and it left scars and distortions upon his personality.

Several striking features of Mendele's writing hint at the grievous effects upon him of his disrupted early life: his strong feeling for children—especially those bereaved, impoverished, or suffering; fierce hatred for authority of all kinds; and a mocking empathy with adolescents in search of themselves and with grown-ups in a state of delayed adolescence. On one level, these are signs of trauma stunting emotional growth, of adolescent conflicts not fully worked through.

Mendele was the first Hebrew writer to depict childhood with understanding, particularly in *In the Valley of Tears* and *Of Bygone Days*. Much of his life was devoted to children, either as a teacher or an administrator. Among his foremost concerns was the education of children; in fact, his first published work, the 'Letter on Education', deals with this issue.[8] In its attack on authoritarianism, the letter anticipates much of Mendele's later work. A good teacher, he insists, does not use anger and blows but enters the child's world, a point repeated in 'The Calf': 'Do you want to know the world of a child? Go, enter his world, become a child yourself, act as you did when you were small' (357). A child's failure to learn, he argues in a radical departure from the accepted norms of the time, is more likely a reflection of the teacher's shortcomings or his poor methods of instruction than of stupidity or recalcitrance on the child's part.

---

[8] Shalom Ya'akov Abramowitz, 'Mikhtav al devar hachinukh' (Letter on Education), *Hamagid*, 1/31 (1857), 121–2. Repr. in *Mishpat shalom* (Judgement of Peace), (Vilna, 1860).

The letter was written in the winter of 1856–7, after Mendele had qualified as a government teacher and was teaching children in Kamenets-Podolsk. In distress over his failed marriage, he must have contemplated how different his life might have been had his childhood and education not been disrupted. The letter might therefore indicate Mendele's wish to make up for his fragmented upbringing and education by devoting himself to the education of children. There was, of course, much need for this work at a time when reform in education and in attitudes towards children was inevitable. Childhood in the Pale, he writes, was little more than a 'passing shadow' (12), and children were horribly unnatural, 'artificial flowers in a woman's hat' (379); they were weighed down by poverty and anxiety, old before their time. Mendele stood out in his lifelong concern and zeal for them.

Mendele's unusually bitter antagonism towards authority might also be linked in part to the father's death. The rage naturally provoked by the death of Reb Chaim would have been the harder for Mendele to work through as his relationship with his father had been strained. Fathers in Mendele's writings are generally respected and feared, but not loved. In *Of Bygone Days*, Reb Chaim is preoccupied with his affairs and has little time for his family: 'Except for Sabbath and holidays he did not take meals with his family' (279). Himself a victim of childhood loss and family disruption,[9] Reb Chaim made his dour authority felt at home. 'Reb Chaim never laughed. He didn't say much, even at home. The children would play boisterously in his absence. No sooner did he set foot in the house than they all fell silent' (290). Similarly, Hirshl's father in *In the Valley of Tears* is permanently choleric, he hardly speaks with his family and never plays with the children. As a result of this treatment, both Shloyme and Hirshl are as wild, mischievous, and loud out of doors as they are repressed at home (150, 268). The father's oppressive influence and, later, his death drive both children into a world of make-believe, 'a delightful, fragrant garden of Eden' where angels sing of hope and love (176), 'the plains of Eden, home of peace, light and joy' (285), by means of which crippling anxiety, depression, and anger might be evaded.

Mendele's anti-authoritarianism is evident also in his view of nature as being at odds with his upbringing: this may be seen in what is perhaps his earliest memory, related in the Introduction to *Of Bygone Days*. For in common with some of the early Romantics, he believed in

---

[9] Weinreich, 'Mendeles eltern un mitkinder', 274.

his innate animal goodness and insight as a child, enabling him to perceive and respond to the awesome, mystical revelation of God's presence on earth, to be at one with nature. All this was crushed by his life in society—this idea brings Rousseau in particular to mind—by the incomprehension of adults, by the father's slap and the mother's admonition.

It happened one spring day. Suddenly it got dark. A little boy came running down the garden path through green shrubs and grass. He came barefoot and naked except for a linen shirt and cap. He would stop, then start running again, eyes roving, ears pricked up like a rabbit. I am that child. At that moment I first became conscious of myself and astonished at everything. There was no other living thing, only the sky above and the earth below, like two fences enclosing me. Suddenly the sky exploded, thunder rolled from one end of the earth to the other, shattering echoes everywhere. Fire dragons and seraphs shot back and forth. 'It's the sound of God's chariot and angels', I thought. 'The Lord of Hosts riding the skies, cracking his whip, slicing blades of flame.' A pillar of dust and straw rose from the earth, twirling like a wheel, rolling in flight from the storm. Another instant and the rain came, warm, good for the earth, reviving the spirit, pelting the plants. Grass and onions and the tender garlic crouched like little children against their mother's breast, drenched in pleasure. Rivulets were everywhere, burbling sweetly to one another, coming together in one stream, foaming noisily. And the great awesome wheel of God's chariot appeared, half-visible—a rainbow in the clouds. It was beautiful. Light spread to the end of the sky. The sun came out groom-like from his cloud-canopy, winking at the clouds—they blushed . . . For the first time I was aware of myself, of God and his earth. Insight from thunder and lightning, understanding from storm. A memory engraved in my mind, never to be forgotten. With my innocent child's heart, I understood the vision and the language of the natural world around me, I knew the speech of plants and garden seedlings, the song of running water, the croak of frogs sunk to the neck in a muddy pool blinking their great eyes—I knew it well, I replied with a good-hearted croak of my own. And when I came to the courtyard of my home and the calf came from the shed and stretched, lowering its head, raising its tail and mooing, and the hen came out of a corner with her chicks, pecking at trash-heaps, scratching and chirping, and the rooster strutted beside them, making eyes and crowing; and I saw the cat come out from under the roof, lean against the wall, leap, miaow—I knew all these and I answered each in its own language, mooing, miaowing, chirping loudly. But the blow that father landed on my cheek—I didn't know what it was or why, and why mother yelled at me when she saw me at the doorway, wet with rain. What they wanted then and what my teachers and others wanted afterwards—I found hard to understand. (257–8)

This memory appears to symbolize a good deal of Mendele's stormy life—his semi-religious devotion to the 'light of Haskalah', his creative imitation of nature, his residual unhappiness with early family and social life. This dissatisfaction might of course have been displaced from later emotions stemming from the father's death and the family's break-up. But the father's slap (as well as the rebuke of mother and teachers) might also be taken as a 'screen memory'[10] representing a whole slice of Mendele's childhood and his relationship with his father.

Much in Mendele's creative life might be interpreted as a slap in the face of authority, a reaction against his father's harsh character and outlook as he experienced or perceived it. This reaction was made more intense and complex by the father's death just as Mendele approached adolescence. (Puberty began about four years later in the 1840s than it does today.[11]) Anger at the lost parent—a normal part of grief[12]—heightened, at times perhaps to a pathological degree, the adolescent rejection of authority. Mendele, an intelligent, gifted orphan whose parental world had failed him and who saw little point in conforming to traditional Jewish society, was a ripe candidate for Haskalah.

Haskalah views on education, nature, religion, and sexual relationships might have attracted Mendele partly because of their anti-authoritarian, anti-establishment, and specifically anti-rabbinic character. His father had wanted him to be an orthodox rabbi and, as pointed out, was so stubbornly opposed to Haskalah that he broke up his daughter's marriage when he found that his son-in-law had Haskalah leanings (290). The rejection of authority extends to God, who is described in *Of Bygone Days* as exacting and irascible (294), much as the father is, and who is blasphemously attacked by the Devil in *The Mare*. The narrator of *The Mare* seems at times to be, as William Blake wrote of Milton, 'of the Devil's party', for he sees God as little better than a communal official, petty and corrupt (330). The Devil, in contrast, has deep insight into evil and how to overcome it: in this respect he brings to mind other villains in Mendele, such as Isaac-Abraham in *The Parasite* and Feibush in *The Beggar Book*.

[10] See ch. 2, n. 4.
[11] Gordon Lowe, *The Growth of Personality: From Infancy to Old Age*, Pelican edn. (London, 1977), 153.
[12] See John Bowlby, *Loss: Sadness and Depression*, vol. iii of *Attachment and Loss* (London, 1980); also Colin Murray Parkes, *Bereavement: Studies of Grief in Adult Life* (London, 1986).

I have pointed out that in his attacks on communal leaders, Mendele singles out the tax collectors, and that his father was a tax collector. His play *The Tax* is his most bitter attack on the meat-tax and on the community officials who used it for their personal gain. The town officials of Berdichev, where Mendele lived in the 1860s, were so enraged by Mendele's transparent indictment of their corruption—we do not have their side of the story—that they virtually forced Mendele and his family to leave town.[13] *The Mare*, written just two or three years later, shows no sign of recantation. To the contrary. The fourth commandment of the Devil's Decalogue, which all 'do-gooders' must observe fastidiously, is a sly parody of the biblical story of the creation of Eve and the institution of marriage.

Be friendly with the powerful. Particularly tax collectors. They are the *primum mobile* of society, source of all good, bone of your bones, flesh of your flesh. Therefore shall the wise man leave his father and mother and God, and cleave to this tax-collector, and they shall speak with one voice and be one. (347)

Whether or not Mendele's father was himself corrupt is a moot question. As meat-tax collector, he had opportunity to abuse his position. The facts that the Kopyl townspeople did not help his family after his death (293) and that he was remembered with hatred (296) suggest that even if he had not been dishonest or cruel, he was regarded as such by some. Mendele casts no doubt on his father's integrity. Yet he might have seen his father as 'bad' or 'corrupt' in that Reb Chaim had treated him and the rest of the family in a cruel, authoritarian way, especially at the end of his life (290), and that he had 'failed' and 'abandoned' his son by dying at a crucial time in the latter's development, when he badly needed a father's guidance and support. The unresolved, distended hatred and revulsion provoked by the father and his death found a natural outlet in Mendele's caricature and satire of communal officials. Their wickedness, which in some cases was real enough, was exaggerated to match and to justify the intensity of the hatred which he needed to let off.

Judging from *Of Bygone Days*, Mendele was in any case rebelling against his father at the time of his death. He had begun to repudiate his father's harsh authority and religious fanaticism. (It is striking that he gives no account of his *bar mitzvah*.) Passionate by nature, he was inflamed by the Evil Inclination which awakened in him in late childhood and drawn to nature, to art and friendship, away from the stifling

---

[13] Klausner, *Historia shel hasifrut ha'ivrit hachadashah*, vi. 350; see p. 43 above.

talmudic world of the past, against his father's wishes. His friendships hinted at the direction in which he was moving. Above all, he preferred the company of his friends Freidl and Ben-Zion and of Ben-Zion's father, Hirzl the carpenter. Hirzl was one of the few eccentrics in Kopyl: he rarely went to synagogue, he played the violin; he made works of art, he had his own garden where he grew fruit and vegetables, he actually owned a dog! Consequently the Kopyl Jews, and probably Reb Chaim too, thought that he was mad. Shloyme, however, 'wanted to be like Hirzl' (287). Shloyme's friendship with Freidl is described immediately before the chapters telling of communal and familial misfortune culminating in Reb Chaim's death. A fire had destroyed the home of Freidl's family, and they temporarily boarded with Reb Chaim and his family. Misfortune was thus Shloyme's good fortune, as he could be with Freidl all the time. In a revealing passage, he pretends to be miserable 'like the heir who appears to weep when his wealthy father dies, but is really happy' (288). As Shloyme's father actually does die soon after, the reader cannot help but conclude that a part of Mendele might have been relieved, if not consciously happy, at the loss of his father.

However, the father's final illness was almost unbearably painful to watch, and the material and psychological consequences of the death were overwhelming. At this vulnerable juncture, as we have seen, Mendele's emotional growth was severely hindered and distorted. He did not have adequate family support, his friendships in Kopyl came to an end, he became increasingly withdrawn and alienated, and his recurrent periods of wandering that continued for several years after the loss point to anxiety, depression, and searching for the lost person. Grief might also have heightened the normal ambivalence of adolescence: anger and rebellion against the father as well as empathy and identification with him. The wish to rebel would have increased to the extent that Mendele was angry at him for dying and relieved at being free of his harsh authority. But in so far as the loss caused him to identify himself with his father, perhaps as an expression of a not-uncommon wish to recover the lost person,[14] the negative emotions arising from the death would have led to guilt and depression.

At any rate, the quest for male identity is a recurrent theme in Mendele's writings and it, too, might be linked in part with the father's death. After he begins to recover from his loss, Shloyme in *Of Bygone*

---

[14] Cf. Bowlby, *Loss: Sadness and Depression*, and C. M. Parkes, *Bereavement*.

Days hungers after friendship and love. He admits his suspicion that his friendships were driven by the Evil Inclination—source of all emotional direction, both good and bad—and describes himself as sinking in a moral swamp. Close male friendships verging on homosexuality, confusion over sexual roles, and the search for male identity figure blatantly in other of Mendele's works, notably *The Travels of Benjamin the Third* and *The Mare*. The friendship, or rather 'marriage', between Benjamin and Senderel in *The Travels of Benjamin the Third* is the most extraordinary, though a similar 'marriage' exists between Mendele and Leib in 'Earthquake Days'. Here, the quest for identity is no less real for being distorted and satirized. The story begins with Benjamin, a man with a wife and children, undergoing a crisis in which he withdraws from his family: 'he wandered alone at night, he sometimes disappeared for hours, he slept alone in the ruin in his yard . . . he stopped seeing and hearing what was in front of him' (60, 62). Intent on proving himself a man, belatedly, by making the hard trek to the Land of Israel, he devotes himself to an ideal of tough masculinity diametrically opposed to his nature. He adopts the figure of Alexander the Great as a male model of identification. In order to combat his natural temerity, he tests himself. 'He decided to act bravely, to suppress his nature, to root out all fear from his heart. He forced himself to walk out alone at night, to sleep alone in his room, to go past the city limits, even though it wore him out and made him very scared' (60). Then he finds an ideal 'wife': Senderel the Woman, a malleable and ludicrous *luftmentsch*, henpecked, beaten, and effectively emasculated by his domineering wife, careless of his indignities to the point of masochism, ultimately warm-hearted and loveable. (He is called Senderel the Woman as his wife puts him to work around the house, and he often does women's chores.) Mendele depicts their friendship as a parody of a homosexual 'marriage': Senderel is Benjamin's 'helpmeet' (62), *ezer kenegdo*, as Eve is to Adam (Gen. 2: 20); and the biblical and rabbinic language of sexual desire and union—*teshukah, zivug, hityachadut*—is frequently used to heighten the fun of ribald farce. 'My blood boils and I long for you' (63), *ve'elekha teshukati* (Gen. 3: 16), exclaims Benjamin to Senderel on proposing that they 'elope' together. Senderel's agreement raises Benjamin's ecstasy to new heights in a parody of romantic love not unworthy of Groucho Marx: ' "My soul, the air I breathe, let me kiss you," cried Benjamin as he hugged Senderel the Woman lovingly' (64); and when Senderel pulls out a bundle of coins, his life savings, from his pocket, Benjamin's joy is unbounded: ' "Now, beloved one of my soul, you deserve a kiss on every limb (*kol ever me'evrei gufkha*)," exclaimed Benjamin joyfully, embracing Senderel the Woman and hugging him' (64). On the morning of their departure, Senderel appears disguised as a woman, and once Benjamin ascertains that the bustling figure in skirts and kerchief is not his wife in hot pursuit, he brightens up and gazes at Senderel like a groom at his beautiful bride, *kekhalah na'ah be'einei dodah* (65). They fairly sail along until Senderel gets tired (66), as a woman does according to the Talmud, *tash kocho kinekevah* (Ber. 32b). To his everlasting credit, Senderel had busied himself like a 'woman of valour', an *eshet chayil* [Prov. 31: 10], to prepare food for the way (67), unlike Benjamin whose preoccupations are masculine and spiritual— until he gets hungry. Each declares his inexorable attraction to the other, Senderel revealing that he was drawn to Benjamin 'like a blind man . . . like a calf after the cow' (67), and Benjamin declaring: 'Our marriage was made in heaven. You and I are body and soul' (ibid.). When they reach Kesalon, they stroll through the streets like a honeymoon couple, 'like a bride and groom during the seven days of feasting after the marriage, alone together, walking in the gardens, enjoying one another's every word and glance' (80).

In *The Mare*, Israel's goal, like that of Benjamin, is to assert his male identity, 'to be a man' (309, 318). In the throes of madness, his reflections on the transmigration of souls, such as that undergone by the mare, transparently reveal the shakiness of his own sexual identity: 'If the mare is a prince,' he thinks to himself, 'I, a male, in contrast, am a princess' (315). He imagines that in a former incarnation he might have been the Queen of Sheba (ibid.). His paranoid suspicion that he is being controlled by an invisible power recalls Benjamin's conviction that he is influenced by such a power (79): in both cases, latent homosexuality might be involved. Just as Benjamin identifies himself with Alexander the Great in order to compensate for the weakness in his male identity, so also Israel links himself through transmigration of souls with Judah Maccabeus, a comparable image of exaggerated masculinity. Longing to prove himself sexually, Israel cannot easily do so even by fantasizing himself into the Devil's party, where sexual licence is rife, for he is terrified that sexual indulgence might drive him mad—if it has not done so already. The Devil in Mendele, one suspects, owes much of his power to the upheavals of childhood and adolescence which, as in the case of the orphaned Israel in *The Mare*, hinder and distort the quest for identity. Having been failed in childhood by the divine forces of justice and order, the orphan is vulnerable to 'demonic possession'.

In many ways, then, Mendele's loss of his father and the poor conditions which followed decisively affected his writings, both realistic and satiric. His art is an exploration of self-image as well as of Jewish identity and, as we shall see in the Conclusion, one is virtually the mirror-image of the other.

Conclusion: An Interpretation of the Origins of Bias

OUR exploration of diverse interwoven strands of realism, social criticism, Jewish self-hate, satire, and autobiography in Mendele shows that while his portrait of the Jews is based solidly on historical truth, it is also saturated with bias. To an extent, this bias was general among Hebrew writers at the time, influenced by social factors such as antisemitism, censorship, Haskalah aims, conventional literary stereotyping, and the backwardness of nineteenth-century Russia. In Mendele's case, however, it seems also to have come from personal pathology, of which he was at least partly aware.

In the sixty-year span of his career, Mendele changed, as did Russian Jewry, in character, outlook, and style. His image went through a unique metamorphosis, from the zealous, controversial *maskil* of the 1850s and 1860s to the wise, beloved 'grandfather' of Yiddish and Hebrew fiction by the turn of the century. His portrayal of the Jews reflects these changes in him: from outright satire and propaganda in *Fathers and Sons*, for example, he moved increasingly in the direction of social realism, particularly in *Of Bygone Days* which, among other things, is an invaluable memoir for historians.

Yet the cumulative picture of the Jews in Mendele's writings, we have seen in Chapter 3, is of a people degraded and corrupt, unchanging and virtually unchangeable. While individual Jews often conflict with the stereotype, the faceless Jewish masses are the target of caricature and generalization. Even in the latter part of Mendele's career, his childhood memories remained the basis for his depiction of the Jews. Of his three major post-1881 works, two are set in the reign of Nicholas I. The early impressions of Jewish suffering and humiliation permeate his fiction. In other ways, too, Mendele's perception of the Jews was limited. He lived all his life in the Pale of Settlement except for brief visits to the Russian interior and a two-year stay in Geneva after the Odessa pogrom of 1905. He knew hardly anything about Jews outside the Pale—admittedly, over half the world Jewish population— and he had little experience of the rich variety of Jewish life elsewhere. Though he writes of a universal Jewish 'character', Jews of Western

Europe and the Orient do not in fact figure in his works, and he writes about the world of the Russian *shtetl* as if it constituted the entirety of Jewish existence.

His lifelong view of the Jews as quintessential beggars was formed by childhood and adolescent observation and experience and reinforced during his stay in Berdichev (1858–69), where there were an exceptionally large number of Jewish paupers. Later, Odessa, with its comparatively prosperous and enlightened atmosphere, impelled him to regard his former life with a certain distance and repugnance and to depict satirically the beggar-Jews whom he had known in the heart of the Pale.

In the early part of his career, as a leading *maskil* Mendele was strongly disposed to place blame for the Jews' degradation and corruption squarely upon the Jews themselves, even where this blame was unwarranted or exaggerated (though not so much after 1881). The Haskalah aimed to expose and, through education, to change the 'negative identity' of the Jews, the narrow and grotesque in Jewish existence, and pave the way to emancipation. In their reforming zeal, the *maskilim* often lost their sense of perspective, in their writings at any rate: they did not emphasize that the Jews were held back by the vile conditions in which they lived, that these conditions prevailed to a greater or lesser extent throughout Europe, and that Russia in particular was so backward that the Jews were advanced in comparison.

The tension between the Haskalah and Jewish orthodoxy made the *maskilim* more receptive than they might otherwise have been to the influence of stereotypes forced on the Jews by Christian society. The Haskalah roused fear among the more orthodox Jews that their traditions would be undermined. Many *maskilim*, Mendele included, were ostracized or even expelled by their communities. The hatred which they stirred up convinced them still further that the Jews surrounding them were narrow and backward. Feeling isolated and trapped, they were often driven to increase their attacks on Jewish society and their struggle to gain secular education and to assimilate into the gentile world. Satire was one of their strongest weapons and underwent much refinement in the battle for reform: indeed, it became the most highly developed Hebrew literary genre in the nineteenth century.[1]

Hebrew satire inevitably set among its targets Jewish characteristics

---

[1] In the last half of the 19th cent. about 70 parodic satires of Russian Jewish life appeared in Hebrew. See I. Davidson, *Parody in Jewish Literature* (New York, 1966), 84.

already exaggerated and deformed by social conditions, the effects of living under a hostile, totalitarian regime. Mendele feared the government—with reason, especially after his son's exile to Siberia. He was also dependent on government approval, first as a teacher and author of Hebrew textbooks and later as headmaster in Odessa. He was wary of expressing consistent political views though, as we have seen, inconsistency came naturally to him. Censorship stymied open blame of the government for the conditions of the Jews in the Pale and, indeed, for the existence of the Pale. Christians are neither villains nor targets of satire in Mendele's writings. While alcoholism, for example, was endemic among the Russian peasants, the only drunk in Mendele's writings is a Jew (146). And though Mendele has grisly accounts of the pogroms in his stories, he never openly blames the rioters, the police, or the government for letting the pogroms break out. The relentless criticism of Russia in Russian literature left its mark on Russian Jewish literature, but if a finger of accusation was to be pointed at anyone, the Jews had to be the victims. For all its liberalism, Russian (and European) literature was in any case dominated by the antisemitic stereotype, and Jewish intellectuals exposed themselves to a severely prejudiced image of the Jews in European civilization. While criticism and satire of the Jews had no trouble passing the censor, viable solutions to the Russian Jewish problem other than assimilation into Russian society are played down, satirized, or dismissed by Mendele: Zionism is little more than a sentimental fantasy or a panicked response in time of emergency; emigration is flight, revolution is taboo. Expressions of Jewish national identity and pride, or protest against antisemitism, are usually muted or disguised in allegory.

Other factors inclining Mendele to bias and distortion in his portrayal of the Jews were two lengthy personal crises which overlapped with the two greatest crises in nineteenth-century Russian Jewish history. The first (*c.*1848–56) began with the death of Mendele's father and the second (*c.*1879–86) with the exile of his son and the death of his beloved daughter, Rachel. After the break-up of his family, the young Mendele was thrust prematurely into the stormy sea of life, as he later described it.[2] Observing the worst of Jewish existence at a most impressionable age, he was predisposed to a distorted self-image and a critical view of the Jews. His naturally critical outlook became sharper and more cynical under the impact of the oppressive laws and

[2] Shalom Ya'akov Abramowitz, dedication of *Hayonekim* (Mammals), vol. i of *Toledot hateva* (Natural History), (Leipzig, 1862), p. viii.

the consequent divisions within the Russian Jewish community during
the reign of Nicholas I. The self-image emerging from Mendele's
autobiographical writings, letters, and the reminiscences of friends is
of a man deeply divided and insecure, and many of the harsh generalizations with which he describes the Jews appear also in self-
descriptions.

The parallels between Mendele and 'the Jews' are manifold: he saw
himself as an archetypal Jew (3), maltreated by others even as the Jews
are abused by the nations,[3] and confessed a sense of inner deformity
not unlike that found in his portrait of the Jews. He too should have
been a prince but, instead, was made into a persecuted mare.

The very fact of my existence betrays a strange error of the Creator or his
angel. Out of Box X he took a soul meant for a well-born man, with full rights
and a free mind, and put it by mistake into some village called Kopyl, put it
golem-like into the womb of some Jewess, honest but poor, dejected, etc. And
so this odd restless creature came into being.[4]

Subjective and critical as he was, Mendele could not easily hold
back the normal human impulse to project one's pain on to others. In a
sense, this was the fountainhead of his artistry and originality. His self-
portrait as a young man in *Of Bygone Days* is, in many ways, a portrait of
the Jewish people—a point made by the writer himself in the Introduction to that work (259). For example, he is full of contradictions,
volatile, chameleon-like (268): so are 'the Jews' (326, 416). He lives in
the past and goes against nature (272): so do 'the Jews' (153, 379). He
is reduced to poverty, degraded, robbed of self-esteem (296): so are
the Jews' (115). His very orphanhood is practically an emblem of
Jewish existence (326). He is in search of manhood and identity (279):
so are 'the Jews', as implied in *The Mare*. He is besmirched by
materialism and thinks more about his stomach than about his soul
(304–5): the same is true of 'the Jews' (391). He writes of himself as a
tired horse (305), the symbol of 'the Jews' in *The Mare*.

I have put much stress on the fact that Mendele began to write
during the period of depression, confusion, uncertainty, and alienation
following his father's death. The 'satanic' impulse to satire, as he
describes it (3), which later found a vehicle in the character of Mendele
the Bookpeddler, began at this time. (Klausner, incidentally, described

---

[3] Letter to Judah Leib Binstock, 16/28 May 1882, National Library Archives,
Jerusalem.
[4] Ibid., 12/24 Dec. 1882.

Mendele as 'Mephistophelean'.[5]) It seems that Mendele was first drawn to satire not as a tool of social criticism as much as a means of satisfying emotional needs linked in part to his father's death. Through satire, Mendele could unleash some of the anger, ambivalence, and hatred of authority arising from, or exaggerated by, the loss of his father. All these emotions fill Mendele's portrayals of the Jews. Loss need not have led directly to Mendele's grotesque satires, but it certainly inclined him in that direction.

I have also emphasized the chronic subjectivity that led Mendele to see the Jews primarily in negative terms, to regard them collectively as beggars much as they are in his stories, and to revile the Jews and Judaism with the venom of an antisemite. Almost always, he treats the failings of individual Jews as symptoms of the vile general character of 'the Jews': for example, in *The Parasite*, Isaac-Abraham blames his criminal nature upon the evil rampant in Jewish society; in *Fathers and Sons*, Ben-Aryeh connects his personal corruption with the alleged decline and fall of the Jews (47); the wickedness of individual Jews is projected on to 'the Jews' in *The Travels of Benjamin the Third* (85) and *In the Valley of Tears* (226–7).

At the same time, many passages in Mendele—for example, *The Beggar Book* (128–9), 'Earthquake Days' (415), and 'Warsaw 1881' (434)—show that he was acutely sensitive to the mechanism of projection. In 'Earthquake Days', Mendele rebukes himself for projecting personal faults and misconceptions on to others: 'You base your judgement and treatment of people on fleeting moods of anger and excitement. So a henpecked preacher might threaten his congregation with the seven fires of Gehenna. Or a flea-bitten writer might challenge the world . . .' (415). In 'Warsaw 1881', the 'Jewish question' is attacked as being a cesspool for the filthy and perverse in human nature, for those with an axe to grind.

To a very large degree, then, Mendele knowingly projected elements of his own pathology on to the Jews. Insecure, ambivalent, low in self-esteem, unbalanced by childhood trauma, he found an outlet in his depiction of the Jews while also throwing into sharp relief the all-too-real contradictions and ironies of Jewish existence. In *Of Bygone Days* (297), he describes the violent yoking of conflicting feelings as the mainspring of art: this was true of Mendele. His later career is implicitly tied to his dual feelings which welled up after his father's death,

---

[5] Klausner, *Historia shel hasifrut ha'ivrit hachadashah*, vi. 388.

when he came back to Kopyl for the High Holy Days to find that his father's seat in synagogue had been sold:

Grief-stricken, ashamed, Shloyme came home and half-heartedly said the holiday blessing in a song of lament . . . As much as he struggled to beat back his despair, to be happy and not profane the holiness of the day, he failed. The opposite happened. A strange face—laughing and furious, like a wafer smeared with honey and vinegar, a sunbeam fighting to break through dark clouds and mists in the rain season. (297)

The Jews are described in much the same way in 'Shelter from the Storm', futilely struggling to rejoice on the festivals. Their powerful effect on Mendele may be ascribed in part to his childhood memory of heartbreak on a Jewish holiday while pretending to be happy:

Not even the sight of Jews sobbing on the Ninth of Av afflicts me like their recital of the *Akdamut millin*[6] on Shavuot. They sing it with such joy, and it does after all promise them a better, more dignified, happier life. It invites them to feast on the Leviathan in the World to Come! They imagine themselves eating and drinking like princes, lovingly served by [God's] ministers— at a time when, in fact, they are sick and ragged with poverty and anxiety, hated, despised and oppressed by all. (384)

In other ways, too, Mendele's portrayal of the Jews might have been affected by unresolved emotions stemming from his loss and the poor conditions for mourning which followed. The Jews, like himself a bundle of contradictions (268, 416), provoke unusual extremes of mockery and love, laughter and tears, anger and acceptance, disgust and empathy: for example, in *The Beggar Book* (93), *Of Bygone Days* (257), *The Mare* (313), 'No Peace for Jacob' (398), 'Earthquake Days' (407, 412), 'The Fire-Victims' (445–6), and elsewhere. A typical illustration might be taken from *The Mare*, in which the Jew, much like Mendele himself, is a figure of contrasts, being both aristocrat and orphan, 'king and worm—honey and wormwood, wine and vinegar, mixed'. 'The orphan's perpetual degradation, the groom's momentary glory' (326). The extremes of Mendele's ambivalence towards the Jews are remarkable: in one passage he might offer a caricature reminiscent of an antisemitic cartoon; in another he feels such rage, protest, and compassion for his suffering people that he would like to do away with

---

[6] *Akdamut millin* ('Introduction'): opening words of an Aramaic poem recited in the synagogue on Shavuot (Pentecost). Mendele's description of the Jews struggling to be appropriately happy on Shavuot may be compared with Elie Wiesel's account in *Night* of the Jews of Sighet shortly before their deportation to Auschwitz.

them; in yet another, overwhelmed with pity for his people, he wants to embrace and kiss them all. The pattern of rejection and identification also appears to underlie Mendele's creative impulse, as seen in *Of Bygone Days*. Shloyme's act of driving away the boy who so closely resembles himself after his father's death impels him, out of guilt and empathy, to write his memoirs.

In short, Mendele's adolescent experience of indigence and wandering might account in no small part for his view of the Jews as beggars and of his self-image as an impoverished 'Jew of Jews'. The impression made by this experience is comparable with that made upon Dickens in the blacking factory.[7] Over thirty-five years after the event, Mendele was still dreaming of beggars.[8] His personal trauma following his father's death appears in fragments in the nightmares of his protagonists, such as those of Israel in *The Mare* and Mendele in 'Warsaw 1881'. In these nightmares, the personal sorrows deriving from loss are linked symbolically to collective trauma.

In *The Mare*, Israel's nightmare of being a sacrificial cock (320–1) reflects his struggle to be a man, to assert his male identity: *gever* in Hebrew means both 'cock' and 'man'.[9] As seen previously, Israel's orphanhood appears to underlie his difficulty in launching out into life. Israel believes that by passing his examinations, entering university, and qualifying as a doctor, he will achieve manhood. His failure in the examination is therefore a crushing blow to his male ideal, a form of castration. For this reason, apparently, on the night after his failure he has the nightmare of being a sacrificial cock, this symbolically denoting castration. However, the concept of castration pertains not only to Israel's personal psychopathology but also to the allegorical scheme of *The Mare*, for the mare is symbol of the Jews—a former prince, emasculated.

Whereas in *The Mare*, Israel's nightmares are part of an allegory of Jewish existence, in 'Warsaw 1881' the juxtaposition of Mendele's nightmares of personal and collective trauma suggests that these are

---

[7] See Edgar Johnson, *Charles Dickens: His Tragedy and Triumph* (Boston, 1952), 31 ff.

[8] Dedication of *Fishke the Lame*, quoted on p. 28 above.

[9] In the description of Israel as a cock (Hirshl is depicted similarly in *In the Valley of Tears*), there may be a hint at Gogol's nefarious parody of Yankel the Jew as a chicken in *Taras Bulba*. However, there is little doubt of Mendele's influence upon S. J. Agnon, whose novel *A Simple Story* also depicts a character who suffers nightmares of being a slaughtered cook. See David Aberbach, 'Breakdown in Mendele and Agnon', *Proceedings of the Ninth World Congress of Jewish Studies* (Jerusalem, 1985).

inseparably linked in his mind. Mendele's nightmares are not unlike those of Israel. He, too, sometimes has reason to doubt his sanity (427). In some ways, he is an older incarnation of Israel: both have lost their fathers and are estranged, in different ways, from the world around them; both are mercurial by temperament and have difficulty in self-control; both are intensely unhappy about traditional Jewish life, with its arranged marriages, excessive mouths to feed and an inability to provide; both represent different stages of the Haskalah—Mendele generally being in favour of Enlightenment, and Israel trying to enter university; both are closely linked with the image of the broken mare, symbolic of their own condition and that of the Jewish people; both loathe the image of the Jewish beggar and *luftmentsch* and imagine themselves, to their horror, flying helplessly through the air; in nightmare both are transformed into animals, Israel into a cock, Mendele into a marmot; to both, nightmare expresses not only their own condition but also that of the Jewish people.

'Warsaw 1881' contains the clearest and most remarkable instance in Mendele's writings of a psychological link between his responses to his father's death and to the pogroms. Emerging from hiding after the pogrom, Mendele returns to his hotel and, without washing, tumbles into bed fully clothed, sandals and all, and falls asleep in a sweat. Towards dawn he has the following five-part nightmare, in which the trail of associations moves inexorably from the father's death to the pogroms. The Warsaw pogrom has clearly triggered off the memory of the father's death with which the nightmare begins.[10]

I didn't recognize myself, where I came from, where I belonged. Eyes shut, ears buzzing, I hurt all over, leaden-limbed, veins throbbing. My mind was chaotic, terrified, confused with weird pictures from my childhood to old age. I saw a leaping he-goat which looked like a child with no trousers or shoes, only a shirt and lambskin hat. It taunted a little boy, set its dog on him, threw stones at him. The child cried—the cry of Mendele. I cried. I suffered. Beaten for nothing. Screaming in terror, I ran to the safety of father's house. I found him, a heap of bones on a straw mat covered with a rag. Oy! This—my shelter, rock of my strength, my father in whom I trust! This broken reed—supports a whole family! He provides us with clothes and food! His face is shrunken, his jaw sags, his eyes are dull. His chest rises and falls, shudders and dies away, his breathing grates in his throat.

I mourn, I ache, I'm turned inside out.

The pictures raged on, various, complex, without end. Revelry, carousing,

[10] The first section of this nightmare is quoted on p. 39 above.

the sound of drum and harp, strange sounds like cats in heat. A young cat in white linen came from under a wedding canopy, followed by a great crowd moving swiftly and dancing along: 'Mazal Tov, wretched creature. Live, Mendele, be fruitful and multiply, provide for your children—here is the bread of affliction which our fathers ate . . .' A cry in a cradle, the cries of infants on every side. Wrath and trouble all around. Pain, suffering, misfortune without end . . .

My head was numbed, my heart pounded, my veins throbbed.

The pictures rolled on in a fury. The crack of a whip, the clatter of unoiled wheels. A mare slowly drawing a heavy wagon. The splendid Sarah bat Tovim[11] appeared in a crowd of pious women, some of them synagogue dues collectors, learned, modest! All loud, talkative, carrying books of supplication old and new! They held on to me, saying: 'Gather our shame—our books— into your wagon!' All God-fearing, speaking, moaning, whispering all at once, voices grinding mill-like, making the earth shake, bombarding the ears. The wheel screeched, the axle groaned, the wagon turned over. The mare collapsed like a carcass, throat outstretched, eyes bulging, windpipe shrivelled date-like, back inflamed with boils, side shrunken, bones protruding. She quivered and struggled in convulsions, sparse tail flicking, groaning deeply.

Oy, chosen treasure! Oy, my carcass!

Torn tormented creature. Mourners wailed on all corners of the earth, amid ruin and desolation. Round me—chaos. Earth's foundation trembled. Heaven's pillars tottered. I rose like dust, hung in mid-air, an abyss beneath me, a huge void before me. A skull floated before my eyes, dancing like a butterfly, whirling ceaselessly round, vanishing then coming before me, grinding teeth, staring at me. Before I could make sense of it, it disappeared. Then terror struck—sparks of fire, fiery coals shot past like lightning, a great thundering storm began, with meteors, earthquakes and a huge blast of the ram's horn. A paper bridge stretched across the abyss. Crowds of Jews gathered, people of the God of Abraham, torn, afflicted, bent with torment, bearing staffs and begging sacks, scurrying across this bridge of miracles in a confused cacophony of misery, song, screams, talk, argument, complaint. The skull reappeared. It had sidelocks and a beard, a long nose and furrowed forehead, eyes flashing, lip twisted, face scowling. The skull of a Jew—floating in mid-air! No body or bodily form, no hands or feet. A skull alone, carried on the wings of the wind. A thousand terrors, but not that, the worst of all! . . . My flesh crept with fear, my body shuddered, I woke and opened my eyes. (426–7)

This nightmare, which in structure, sophistication and meaning might be compared with some of the dreams in Freud's *Interpretation of Dreams* published a half-decade later, begins with personal loss and

---

[11] Sarah bat Tovim: 17th-cent. authoress who lived in the Polish town of Satanow and composed two Yiddish books of supplications for women.

terror and ends in collective loss and panic. The masses of Jews arouse Mendele's compassion not only because he is one of them but also because their calamity revives his memories of his father's death. The Jew's skull could thus symbolize both the horror of Jewish existence and the dead father. The crowds and the blowing of the ram's horn, the herald of redemption, are linked with a previous nightmare of Mendele's, based on the Talmud (Shab. 88*a*, Av. Zar. 2*b*), in which the Jews are forced to accept the Torah at Sinai (425): what this new Torah entails, however, is not entirely clear. What is clear is that the cataclysm of the pogroms might be a necessary prelude to redemption and the resurrection of the Jews in the Land of Israel. In Mendele's final nightmare in 'Warsaw 1881', the motifs of personal and collective trauma and redemption occur again, this time in the form of a beast-fable strikingly like some of Kafka's stories, such as 'Metamorphosis':

I was a little creature, like a furry coat, short-legged, short-tailed. I crouched on all fours, quietly, confidently. My heart, kidneys and brain were all at rest. Only my stomach was active, digesting its greens. There was nothing in the world but my stomach. It was enough that I was alive. No questions, nothing to puzzle over—not my strange appearance, the means of my subsistence, the reality of my being. Everything was as it should be and that was natural, it was right for me. I crouched, nose protruding, I dozed a bit, breathing through my nose. Then—a voice: 'Look, a marmot, a lovely doormouse. Let's hunt it!' I shook the dust off me and shot off into one of the holes. Then I knew—I was a doormouse, a tiny, weak creature of the whistling marmot species. In the hole I found a large crowd of brother doormice, some blind and lame, ribs crushed, legs smashed, hair and tails ripped out. We marmots like to laze and sleep and dream. I joined the sleeping crowd and dropped off. We slept and dozed, then the hunters' voices reached us. We woke and took off in all directions, each to his hole or den. I joined one aristocratic group as I heard them saying, 'Let's go to the Cave of Machpelah [the burial place of the Patriarchs in Hebron]. It's a good, spacious cave in rock crevices. We'll be alright there.' We all went in a commotion through caves, and I brought up the rear. The way was dark and slippery. Some fell into pits and didn't come out again. Others slipped, writhing, and saved themselves by the skin of their teeth. I too was in mortal danger, there were so many hardships and blows. My body was a mass of bruises, my skin was frozen, I was hungry and tired, limping on one thigh. Still, we didn't turn back. Soon we would come to the cave. Stealthily, a little further, a little courage, to break through a little hole. We discussed strategy, and in the end decided to line up and enter the hole, shoved and choking, one by one. When my turn came, I stuck my head in the hole. The doormouse behind me pushed with all his might. The pain was so great that I did what my species does in emergencies—I whistled long and loud. (436–7)

The immediate trigger of this nightmare is the discussion of the Jewish question among a group of Jews with whom Mendele shares a dormitory in Warsaw. One of these men, Segal, gives a fierce and eloquent attack on the idea of the 'Jewish question', which he sees as an expression of antisemitic psychopathology. Yet his words are strangely apt also in relation to Mendele's art.

The Jewish question has becomes a cesspool for all the filth, shit and vomit of the human heart. The filth pours down, following the law of gravity, and as long this goes on—human nature being what it is, there will be no end of it—and the Jews remain impoverished and low in status, they will always be the cesspool of mankind. (434)

Shortly after, Mendele and the others go to sleep, and at this point, amid a cacophony of snoring, Mendele has his nightmare in which he is forced by instinct to Zionism. Plunged into self-consciousness and action by persecution, not ideology, Mendele is driven like a hunted beast through underground caverns—as in the Jewish legend of the resurrection at the end of days (Gen. Rab. 96: 5)—to the Land of Israel and the Cave of Machpelah. He is also implicitly compared with Jacob limping after wrestling with the angel, for he too has been wounded and transformed. Yet, the final image in the nightmare, of being trapped, neither in nor out, appears to symbolize Mendele's state of being in two minds over the Zionist solution.

The pogroms loom large over Mendele's portrait of the Jews. It is of psychological interest that Mendele the Bookpeddler responds to the pogroms much as Shloyme reacts to his father's death, with a sense of alienation from nature:[12] 'Everything I saw looked strange and foreign: the forests, the fields, had all changed utterly' (406); 'the sky turned dark, the woods lost their majesty' (293).

Collective trauma in normal conditions—for example, in an unavoidable natural disaster, an earthquake or flood—is known to have an overwhelming, longlasting impact on the survivors. The pogroms of 1881–4 were more devastating than catastrophe in normal times. Their proportions were staggering: as many as one hundred thousand Jews were directly affected by the violence and vandalism and, after the May Laws of 1882, a million and a half living in rural areas were driven into the cities of the Pale; about two million emigrated. The Jews had no support from the government but, on the contrary, were blamed for bringing the pogroms upon their own heads.

[12] See pp. 43, 88 above.

Most of Mendele's fiction, both in Yiddish and Hebrew, was written after the pogroms. He had devoted his life to the struggle for enlightenment and progress, but before his eyes Russia was going back to the Dark Ages. Now the need to cope with and give expression to massive trauma became dominant in Mendele's creativity. Personal bitterness and protest deriving mostly from childhood upheaval were exacerbated by the pogroms and by the personal tragedies which occurred at this time. In his letters of 1881–2, Mendele writes that the pogroms and his daughter's death had silenced him.[13] The silence was broken explosively in the Hebrew stories he wrote starting in 1886 with 'Shelter from the Storm'. The story marks Mendele's return to Hebrew fiction after eighteen years and the first appearance of Mendele the Bookpeddler in Hebrew fiction. The pogroms—the 'storm' in the title— were clearly a factor in bringing Mendele back to Hebrew fiction. The Hebrew short stories which he wrote over the next decade, though often enlivened with satiric humour, have a leaden maturity, an almost unbearable weight of sorrow which sets them apart from all previous Hebrew literature.[14]

Though set in a particular time and place, Mendele's art does not belong to Jewish literature alone, but is an integral part of Russian and European literature. By describing the Russian Jews, he also gives an oblique picture of Russia and its failure to adapt to the pressure for change which eventually led to revolution. His portrayal of the Jews is typically double-edged, as it foreshadows calamity yet offers hope. In some respects, his writings point the way to Auschwitz: inasmuch as the Holocaust is regarded by many historians as a culmination of the history of antisemitism in which the tsarist government played a major part, Mendele's depiction of the effects of this hatred upon the Russian Jews cannot be detached from the historical and psychological processes that permitted genocide. Yet in capturing the weakness and shame of

---

[13] Letters to Judah Leib Binstock of 17/29 Nov. 1881 and 24 Jan./5 Feb. 1882; National Library Archives, Jerusalem.

[14] A parallel change may be detected in other Hebrew writers of the time, such as Peretz Smolenskin, Reuben Asher Braudes, Moses Leib Lilienblum, and the satirist Joseph Brill. On the latter, see Davidson, *Parody in Jewish Literature*. The shift from satire to social allegory had begun in works written prior to the pogroms, but became especially pronounced afterwards. See Ruth R. Wisse, *The Schlemiel as Modern Hero* (Chicago, 1971), ch. 2. On Mendele's literary response to the pogroms, see Alan Mintz, *Hurban: Responses to Catastrophe in Hebrew Literature* (New York, 1984); and David Roskies, *Against the Apocalypse: Responses to Catastrophe in Modern Jewish Culture* (Cambridge, Mass., 1984).

the Jews—all the more effectively with an ugly streak of malice and bias—Mendele warned of their susceptibility to the prejudices and pathological hatred of their enemies. As a result, he had much influence on the early Zionists, who regarded his works as a powerful justification for the return to the Land of Israel. For all his ambivalence towards the Jewish people, his work was seen, not unjustly, as an indirect declaration of independence, part of a growing wave of national feeling during and after the pogroms.

Mendele's angry pessimism, mockery, and self-hate served to goad the Jews into facing their crippled condition and to taking action to change their lives. He thus helped to open the way to a redefinition of Jewish identity in national as opposed to religious terms. Perhaps equally important was the effect on Jewish morale of the perfection of his art, first in Yiddish then in Hebrew. By creating the first works of lasting literary importance in modern Yiddish, Mendele became the first modern Yiddish writer to overcome his disdain for the language. Through an astonishing feat of creative alchemy, he then succeeded in transforming his Yiddish classics into Hebrew. In so doing, he produced a body of work worthy of comparison with some of the finest European literature of the time, and gave an incalculable spur to the growth of Hebrew. For all these reasons, Mendele is a key figure in modern Jewish literature, a satirist and realist of deep intelligence and complexity in whom laughter and tears were mingled, who, while cruelly exposing his people, warts and all, gave inadvertent expression to their power to endure and to prevail.

Bibliography

WORKS BY MENDELE

Yiddish and Hebrew Editions

THE main edition used in the present study is the one-volume *Kol kitvei Mendele Mocher Sefarim* (Collected Works of Mendele Mocher Sefarim), (Tel Aviv, 1947). On the contents of this volume, see the 'Note on Texts' in the Introduction. Other editions consulted include *Kol kitvei Mendele Mocher Sefarim (S. Y. Abramowitz)* (Collected Works of Mendele Mocher Sefarim) [in Hebrew], 3-vol. Jubilee edn. (Cracow–Warsaw–Odessa, 1909–12), and *Ale verk fun Mendele Mocher Sefarim* (Collected Works of Mendele Mocher Sefarim) [in Yiddish], 8 vols. in 20 pts. (Warsaw etc., 1911–13).

The following chronological list of selected works is intended to clarify Mendele's evolution as a Yiddish and Hebrew writer.[1]

(1857)   'Mikhtav al devar hachinukh' (Letter on Education), *Hamagid*, 1/31.

(1860)   *Mishpat shalom* (Judgement of Peace), (Vilna). Critical essays in Hebrew.

(1861)   'Chokhmat hanituach' (Medical Operations), *Hamelitz*, 1/27.

(1862)   *Toledot hateva* (Natural History), vol. i, *Hayonekim* (Mammals), (Leipzig).
——— 'Limdu heitev' (Learn to Do Well), (Warsaw). Mendele's earliest Hebrew fiction; Dan Miron's edition (New York, 1969) includes an Introduction, notes, and supplements.

(1864/5) *Dos kleyne mentschele* (The Parasite), (Warsaw). First appearance of the character of Mendele the Bookpeddler. Translated into Hebrew by Shalom Luria with Introduction and notes (Haifa, 1984). (A second Yiddish version was published in 1879.)

(1865)   *Dos vinshfingerl* (The Magic Ring), (Warsaw). A second version was published in 1888/9.

(1866)   *Toledot hateva*, vol. ii, *Ha'of* (Birds), (Zhitomir).

[1] Derived from S. Werses and Ch. Shmeruk (eds.), *Mendele Mocher Sefarim: Bibliography of his Works and Letters for the Academic Edition* (Jerusalem, 1965).

(1868)   *Ha'avot vehabanim* (Fathers and Sons), (Odessa). Mendele's
         first Hebrew novel, based on 'Limdu heitev' (1862).
         —— *Sefer divrei hayamim livenei haRussim* (History of the Russian
         People) (Odessa). Incomplete translation of a Russian textbook.

(1869)   *Die takse* (The Tax), (Zhitomir). Mendele's first Yiddish play.
         —— *Fishke der Krummer* (Fishke the Lame), (Zhitomir). Trans-
         lated into Hebrew by Shalom Luria in Dan Miron (ed.), Men-
         dele Mocher Sefarim, *Sefer hakabtzanim* (Tel Aviv, 1988). A
         second Yiddish version was published in 1888/9, and a third in
         1907.

(1872)   *Toledot hateva*, vol. iii, *Hazochalim* (Reptiles), (Vilna).

(1873)   *Die kliatsche* (The Mare), (Vilna). A second version was pub-
         lished in 1888/9.

(1875)   'Hagoy lo nikhsaf' (Shameless Nation), *Hamagid*, 19/19–23.
         On antisemitism.

(1878)   'Ahavah le'umit vetoledoteihah' (Nationalism and Its Con-
         sequences), *Hamelitz*, 14/6, 7, 10–12, 15.
         —— *Kitzur masot binyamin hashelishi* (An Abridged Version of
         The Travels of Benjamin the Third), (Vilna).

(1879)   *Dos kleyne mentschele*. New Yiddish version.

(1884)   'A sguleh tsu di yiddishe tsoros' (A Solution to the Jewish
         Problem), (Odessa). Translation of Leon Pinsker's 'Auto-
         emancipation'.
         —— *Der priziv* (The Conscription), (St Petersburg). A play in
         five acts.

(1886/7) 'Beseter ra'am' (Shelter From the Storm), *Hayom*, nos. 41–2;
         Ben ami, Apr.–May, pp. 1–25. Mendele's return to Hebrew
         fiction and first appearance of the character of Mendele the
         Bookpeddler in Hebrew prose.

(1888/9) Publication of new versions of *Dos vinshfingerl*, *Fishke der
         Krummer*, and *Die kliatsche*.

(1890)   'Shem veYefet ba'agalah' (Shem and Japheth in the Train),
         Kaveret (Odessa).

(1892)   'Lo nachat beYa'akov' (No Peace for Jacob), *Pardes*, 1 (Odessa).

(1894)   'Biyemei hara'ash' (Earthquake Days) and Introduction to
         Bayamim hahem (Of Bygone Days), *Pardes*, 2 (Odessa).

(1894–5) 'Biyeshivah shel ma'alah uveyeshivah shel matah' (Warsaw,
         1881); *Luach achiasaf*, 2–3 (Odessa).

(1896)   *Masot Binyamin Hashelishi* (The Travels of Benjamin the
         Third), (Odessa). Mendele's first major artistic achievement in
         Hebrew reworked from a Yiddish original.

―― Start of serialization of *Be'emek habakhah* (In the Valley of Tears), reworked from *Dos vinshfingerl*, in *Hashiloach*, Odessa. (Completed in 1908.)

(1897)   'Hanisrafim' (The Fire Victims), *Pardes*, 3 (Odessa).

(1899)   *Shloyme Reb Chaims*. Autobiography in Yiddish, in *Der yid* (Warsaw).

(1903)   Start of reworking of *Shloyme Reb Chaims* into Hebrew as *Bayamim hahem*, in *Hazeman* (Vilna).

(1907)   *Fishke der Krummer*. New Yiddish version (Odessa).

(1909–12) *Kol kitvei Mendele Mocher Sefarim*, includes Hebrew reworkings of *Dos vinshfingerl*, *Fishke der Krummer*, *Die kliatsche*, and *Shloyme Reb Chaims* as well as *Ha'avot vehabanim*.

(1911–13) *Ale verk fun Mendele Mocher Sefarim.*

English Translations

A list of English translations of Mendele's works is given in Y. Goell, *Bibliography of Modern Hebrew Literature in Translation* (Jerusalem, 1968), nos. 2271–2308, 2831–2. All of Mendele's novels except for *Fathers and Sons* and *In the Valley of Tears* have been translated from the Yiddish, as follows:

The Parasite (Dos kleyne mentschele), tr. G. Stillman (New York, 1956).
The Mare (Die kliatsche), tr. J. Neugroschel, in *Great Works of Jewish Fantasy*, ed. J. Neugroschel (London, 1976).
The Travels and Adventures of Benjamin the Third (Masot binyamin hashelishi), tr. M. Spiegel (New York, 1949).
Fishke the Lame (Fishke der Krummer), tr. G. Stillman (New York, 1960).
Of Bygone Days (Shloyme Reb Chaims), tr. R. Sheindlin, in *A Shtetl and Other Stories*, ed. Ruth R. Wisse (New York, 1973).

Lengthy excerpts of some of these translations (*The Parasite*, *The Mare*, *Fishke the Lame*, *The Travels of Benjamin the Third*, and *Of Bygone Days*) are included, together with translations of *Shem and Japheth in the Train* and *Notes for My Biography*, and a summary of Mendele's life, time, and works, in *The Three Great Classic Writers of Modern Yiddish Literature*, vol. 1, *The Selected Works of Mendele Moykher-Sforim*, ed. Marvin Zuckerman, Gerald Stillman, and Marion Herbst (Malibu, Calif.: Pangloss Press, 1991).

SECONDARY SOURCES

ABERBACH, D., 'Screen Memories of Writers', *International Review of Psycho-Analysis*, 10/1 (1983).
―― 'Breakdown in Mendele and Agnon', *Proceedings of the Ninth World Congress of Jewish Studies* (Jerusalem, 1985).
―― *Bialik* (London, 1988).

ABERBACH, D., *Surviving Trauma: Loss, Literature and Psychoanalysis* (New Haven, Conn., 1989).

AHAD HA'AM, *Igerot* (Letters), ed. A. Simon, 6 vols. (Tel Aviv, 1956–60).

ALTER, R., *The Invention of Hebrew Prose: Modern Fiction and the Language of Realism* (Seattle, 1988).

BABEL, I., *Collected Stories*, tr. W. Morison, Penguin edn. (Harmondsworth, Middx., 1974).

BACK, S., 'Kitvei Mendele Mocher Sefarim kitemunah lechayei Am Yisrael bitekufato' (Mendele's Works as a Portrait of the Jews of His Time), Hebrew University diss., 1976.

BARTANA, O., *Mendele Mocher Sefarim: Iyun bemichlol yetzirato shel Abramowitz* (A Critical Study of Mendele), (Tel Aviv, 1979).

BELINSKY, V. G., *Selected Philosophical Works* (Westport, Conn., 1981).

BELLOW, S., *Mr. Sammler's Planet* (London, 1970).

BERKOWITZ, Y. D., *Harishonim kivenei adam* (Essays), vol. vii of *Kitvei Y. D. Berkowitz* (Collected Works), (Tel Aviv, 1953).

BIALIK, C. N., *Igerot* (Letters), ed. F. Lachower, 5 vols. (Tel Aviv, 1937–9).

—— *Kol kitvei Chaim Nachman Bialik* (Collected Works of Chaim Nachman Bialik), (Tel Aviv, 1958).

BIALIK, C. N. and Y. H. RAVNITZKY (eds.), *Kol kitvei Mendele Mocher Sefarim* (Collected Works of Mendele Mocher Sefarim), vol. iv (pt. 7), 1922.

BINSTOCK, J. L., 'Letoledotav shel Mendele' (Mendele's Life), tr. from Russian by Y. Sofer (J. Klausner), *Hashilo'ach*, 34/1 (1918). (Originally published in *Voskhod*, 1884, no. 12.)

BOROWSKI, T., *This Way to the Gas, Ladies and Gentlemen* [1959], tr. B. Vedder (London, 1976).

BOWLBY, J., *Loss: Sadness and Depression*, vol. iii, *Attachment and Loss* (London, 1980).

BRENNER, J. C., 'Ha'arakhat atzmeinu bisheloshet hakerakhim' (Our Self-Assessment in the Three Volumes [of Mendele's *Collected Works*, 1909–12], 1914, in *Kol kitvei J. C. Brenner* (Collected Works), vol. iii (Tel Aviv, 1967).

CHAPLIN, C., *My Autobiography* (New York, 1966).

CHAZAN, R., and M. L. RAPHAEL (eds.), *Modern Jewish History: A Source Book* (New York, 1974).

COLERIDGE, S. T., *Specimens of the Table Talk*, 4th edn. (London, 1851).

DAVIDSON, I., *Parody in Jewish Literature* (New York, 1966 [1907]).

DIJUR, I. M., 'Jews in the Russian Economy', in J. Frumkin *et al.* (eds.), *Russian Jewry (1860–1917)*, tr. M. Ginsberg (New York, 1966).

DOSTOYEVSKY, F., *Crime and Punishment* [1865–6], tr. D. Magarshak, Penguin edn. (Harmondsworth, Middx., 1966).

—— *The House of the Dead* [1860], tr. D. McDuff, Penguin edn. (Harmondsworth, Middx., 1985).

—— *The Possessed*, tr. Constance Garnett, 2 vols. (London, 1952 [1871–2]).

DUBNOW, S., 'Zikhronot al Mendele Mocher Sefarim' (Reminiscences about Mendele Mocher Sefarim), *Hado'ar*, 21 Mar. (29 Adar), 4 Apr. (14 Nisan), 37/21–2 (1958 [1918]).

—— *History of the Jews*, 5 vols. [1925–9], tr. M. Spiegel (New York, 1967–73).

ELLMANN, R., *Four Dubliners* (London, 1987).

ERIKSON, E., *Identity: Youth and Crisis* [1968] (London, 1974).

FICHMAN, J., 'Be'or hashekiyah' (Mendele's Twilight Years), in *Kol kitvei Mendele Mocher Sefarim* (Collected Works of Mendele Mocher Sefarim), 1922 edn., vol. 4, pt. 7.

FLECK, J., 'Mendele in Pieces', 3/2 *Prooftexts* (1983), 169–88.

FRANKEL, J., *Perush lesusati shel Mendele Mocher Sefarim* (A commentary on Mendele's *The Mare*), (Tel Aviv, 1946).

FREUD, S., *The Interpretation of Dreams*, vols. iv and v of the standard edition of *The Complete Psychological Works of Sigmund Freud*, tr. J. Strachey (London, 1900).

FRISCHMANN, DAVID, 'Mendele Mocher Sefarim', Introd. to *Kol kitvei Mendele Mocher Sefarim* (Collected Works of Mendele Mocher Sefarim), 3 vol. edn. (Warsaw etc., 1909–12).

FRUMKIN, J., G. ARONSON and A. GOLDENWEISER (eds.), *Russian Jewry (1860–1917)*, tr. M. Ginsburg (New York, 1966).

GILMAN, S. L., *Jewish Self-Hatred: Anti-Semitism and the Hidden Language of the Jews* (Baltimore, 1986).

GOGOL, N. *The Collected Tales and Plays of Nikolai Gogol*, ed. L. J. Kent, tr. C. Garnett (New York, 1969).

GORDON, H. L., 'Sichah im Mendele Mocher Sefarim' (A conversation with Mendele), Kressel Archive, Oxford Centre for Postgraduate Hebrew Studies, Yarnton, Oxford.

GOTTLOBER, A. B., *Zikhronot umasa'ot* (Memories and Journeys), ed. E. Goldberg (Jerusalem, 1976).

GREENBERG, L. S., *The Jews in Russia: The Struggle for Emancipation*, 2 vols. (New Haven, Conn., 1965 [1944]).

HALKIN, S., *Modern Hebrew Literature: Trends and Values* (New York, 1950).

HARAMATI, A., *Bedikat hakitrug al Mendele* (An Investigation of the Criticism on Mendele), (Tel Aviv, 1984).

HERLIHY, P., *Odessa: A History, 1794–1914* (Cambridge, Mass., 1986).

HINGLEY, R., *Russian Writers and Society, 1825–1904*, World University Library (New York, 1967).

HUNDERT, G. D., and G. C. BACON, *The Jews in Poland and Russia: Bibliographical Essays* (Bloomington, Ind., 1984).

JOHNSON, E., *Charles Dickens: His Tragedy and Triumph*, 2 vols. (Boston, 1952).

KAFKA, F., *Metamorphosis and Other Stories*, tr. W. and E. Muir, Penguin edn. (Harmondsworth, Middx., 1968).

KARIV, A., *Atarah leyoshenah* (Essays), (Tel Aviv, 1956).

KLAUSNER, J., 'Sichot chulin shel Reb Mendele' (Mendele's Conversation), *Hashiloach*, 34/1 (1918).

—— *Historia shel hasifrut ha'ivrit hachadashah* (History of Modern Hebrew Literature), 6 vols. (Jerusalem, 1952–8).

KRESSEL, G., 'Mendele Mocher Sefarim', in *Leksikon hasifrut ha'ivrit badorot ha'acharonim* (Lexicon of Modern Hebrew Literature), vol. ii (Tel Aviv, 1967).

KUNITZ, J., *Russian Literature and the Jew* (New York, 1929).

KURZWEIL, B., 'Olamo ha'epi shel Mendele' (The Epic World of Mendele), in *Sifrutenu hachadashah: Hemshekh o mahapekhah?* (Modern Hebrew Literature: Continuation or Revolution?), (Tel Aviv, 1959).

LACHOWER, F., *Toledot hasifrut ha'ivrit hachadashah* (History of Modern Hebrew Literature), vol. iii (Tel Aviv, 1944).

LEWIS, B., *Semites and Antisemites: An Inquiry into Conflict and Prejudice* (London, 1986).

LINCOLN, W. B., *Nicholas I: Emperor and Autocrat of All the Russias*, Penguin edn. (Harmondsworth, Middx., 1978).

—— *The Romanovs: Autocrats of All the Russias* (London, 1981).

LOWE, G., *The Growth of Personality: From Infancy to Old Age*, Pelican edn. (London, 1977).

LURIA, S., 'Halashon hafigurativit bitzirato haduleshonit shel Mendele Mocher Sefarim' (Figurative Language in the Bilingual Works of Mendele Mocher Sefarim), (Hebrew University diss., 1977).

MAYZEL, N. (ed.), *Dos Mendele buch* (The Mendele Book), (New York, 1959).

MELAMED, S. M., *Hamitzpeh*, 11/19 (8 May 1914), Kressel Archive, Oxford Centre for Postgraduate Hebrew Studies, Yarnton, Oxford.

MENDES-FLOHR, P. R., and J. REINHARZ (eds.), *The Jew in the Modern World: A Documentary History* (New York, 1980).

MINTZ, A., *Hurban: Responses to Catastrophe in Hebrew Literature* (New York, 1984).

MIRON, D., *A Traveler Disguised: A Study in the Rise of Modern Yiddish Fiction in the Nineteenth Century* (New York, 1973).

—— *Bein chazon le'emet* (Essays on the Development of Modern Hebrew and Yiddish Fiction), (Jerusalem, 1979).

NEIMAN, M., *A Century of Modern Hebrew Literary Criticism, 1784–1884* (New York, 1983).

NIGER, S., *Mendele Mocher Sefarim: Sein Leben, seine Geselschaftlekhe un literaturische Oiftuungen* (Mendele's Life and Literary Achievement), (New York, 1970 [1935]).

PARKES, J., *A History of the Jewish People*, Pelican edn. (London, 1964).

PARKES, C. M., *Bereavement: Studies of Grief in Adult Life* (London, 1986).

PARRISH, R., *Growing Up in Hollywood* (London, 1976).

PATAI, RAPHAEL, *The Arab Mind* (New York, 1983).

PATTERSON, D., *The Hebrew Novel in Czarist Russia* (Edinburgh, 1964).

PERI, M., 'Ha'analogiah umekomah bemivneh haroman shel Mendele Mocher Sefarim' (On Analogies in Mendele's Novels), 1/1 *Hasifrut* (1968).

PINSKER, L., 'Autoemancipation', in Robert Chazan and M. L. Raphael, eds., *Modern Jewish History: A Source Book* (New York, 1974).

PIPES, R., *Russia under the Old Regime* (London, 1974).

POLIAKOV, L., *The History of Antisemitism*, vol. iii, *From Voltaire to Wagner* [1968], tr. M. Kochan (London, 1975); vol. iv, *Suicidal Europe, 1870–1933* [1977] (Oxford, 1985).

RAMBA, I., 'Madu'a hitnatzer beno shel Mendele?' (Why Did Mendele's Son Convert to Christianity?), *Hado'ar*, 28 June (2 Tamuz), 48/32 (1968).

RAVNITZKY, J. H., 'Shalom Ya'akov Abramovitz', in *Kol kitvei Mendele Mocher Sefarim* (Collected Works), 1922 edn., IV. vii. 24–7.

——*Dor vesoferav: Reshimot vedivrei zikhronot al sofrei dori* (Writers I Have Known), 2 vols. (Tel Aviv, 1926, 1937).

RAV TZAIR [Chaim Chernowitz], *Masekhet zikhronot* (Memoirs), (New York, 1945).

ROSKIES, D., *Against the Apocalypse: Responses to Catastrophe in Modern Jewish Culture* (Cambridge, Mass., 1984).

SADAN, D., 'Bishenei nechirav' (Through His Two Nostrils), in *Avnei gader* (Essays on Writers and Books), (Tel Aviv, 1965).

SALTYKOV-SHCHEDRIN, M., *The History of a Town: Or The Chronicle of Foolov* [1869–70], tr. S. Brownsberger (Ann Arbor, 1982).

——*The Golovlets* [1875–80], tr. I. P. Foote (New York, 1986).

SCHOLEM, G., *Major Trends in Jewish Mysticism* [1941], (New York, 1974).

SHAKED, G., *Bein sechok ledemah: Iyunim bitzirato shel Mendele Mocher Sefarim* (Between Laughter and Tears: Studies in Mendele's Works), (Tel Aviv, 1965).

——*Hasiporet ha'ivrit 1880–1970* (Hebrew Narrative, 1880–1970), vol. i (Tel Aviv, 1977).

SHMERUK, C., 'Be'ayot becheker hatekstim shel Mendele beyiddish' (Problems in the Study of Mendele's Yiddish Texts), *Proceedings of the Fourth World Congress of Jewish Studies* (Jerusalem, 1969).

——(ed.), *Chalifat igerot bein S. Y. Abramowitz uvein C. N. Bialik uvein J. H. Ravnitzky* (Correspondence between Abramowitz, Bialik, and Ravnitzky), (Jerusalem, 1976).

SLUTSKY, J., *Ha'itonut hayehudit-Russit bame'ah hatesha esreh* (Russian Jewish Periodicals in the Nineteenth Century), (Jerusalem, 1970).

SREBERK, S. Z., *Zikhronot* (Memoirs), ed. A. Akaviah, S. Z. Sreberk (Tel Aviv, 1955).

STANISLAWSKY, M., *Tsar Nicholas I and the Jews: The Transformation of Jewish Society in Russia, 1825–1855* (Philadelphia, 1983).

STANISLAWSKY, M., *For Whom Do I Toil: J. L. Gordon and the Crisis of Russian Jewry* (New York, 1988).

STEINBERG, T. L., *Mendele Mocher Sefarim* (Boston, 1977).

STERNE, L., *Tristram Shandy* [1760] (New York, 1960).

SZEINTUCH, Y., 'Sipurav haketzarim shel Mendele Mocher Sefarim al nuscha'oteihem' (Mendele's Short Stories and their Versions), *Hasifrut* 1/2 (1968–9).

TALMON, J., 'European History as the Seedbed of the Holocaust', in J. Sonntag (ed.), *Jewish Perspectives: Twenty-five Years of Modern Jewish Writing* (London, 1980).

TOLSTOY, L., *Anna Karenina* [1874–6], tr. R. Edmonds, Penguin edn. (Harmondsworth, Middx., 1968).

TREADGOLD, D. W., *The West in Russia and China*, vol. i, *Russia (1472–1917)*, (Cambridge, 1973).

TROYAT, H., *Gogol: The Biography of a Divided Soul* (London, 1974).

TURGENEV, I., *Fathers and Sons* [1861], tr. R. Edmonds, Penguin edn. (Harmondsworth, Middx., 1965).

WAXMAN, M., *A History of Hebrew Literature* [1941] 5 vols. (New York, 1960).

WEINREICH, M., 'Mendeles eltern un mitkinder' (Mendele's parents and siblings), *YIVO bleter* (1937), no. 11.

WERSES, S., *Bikoret habikoret* (Criticism on Criticism), (Tel Aviv, 1982).

——'Mendele Mocher Sefarim', *Encyclopaedia Judaica*, xi. 1317–23.

——*MiMendele ad Hazaz* (From Mendele to Hazaz), (Jerusalem, 1987).

——*Sipur veshoresho: Iyunim behitpatchut haprozah ha'ivrit* (Studies in the Development of Hebrew Prose), (Ramat Gan, 1971).

WERSES, S., and CH. SHMERUK (eds.), *Mendele Mocher Sefarim*. Bibliography of his Works and Letters for the Academic Edition (Jerusalem, 1965).

WIESEL, E., *Night*, tr. S. Rodway (London, 1960).

WISSE, R. R., *The Schlemiel as Modern Hero* (Chicago, 1971).

ZBOROWSKI, M., and E. HERZOG, *Life Is With People: The Culture of the Shtetl* [1952] (New York, 1974).

ZUCKERMAN, M., G. STILLMAN, and M. HERBST, *The Three Great Classic Writers of Modern Yiddish Literature*, vol. i, The Selected Works of Mendele Moykher-Sforim (Malibu, Calif., 1991).

Index

Abramowitz, Shalom Ya'akov *see*
   Mendele Mocher Sefarim
Ahad Ha'am   45–6
'Ahavah le'umit vetoledoteihah' *see*
   'Nationalism and its Consequences'
Agnon, Samuel Joseph   1, 10, 108 n.
antisemitism, in tsarist Russia
   attacks on, in *The Mare*   50
   background to   1
   and Holocaust, anticipation of
      11
   and Jewish intellectuals, effect on
      104
   and Jewish self-hate   48–64 *passim*
   and population explosion   85
   in Russian literature   52, 104
   and Zionism, in 'Warsaw 1881'   112,
      113
   see also bias; Jews in Russia; pogroms
'Autobiographical Notes' ('Reshimot
   letoledotai')   8, 12, 40, 90, 91

Babel, Isaac   79 n.
Bayamim hahem see Of Bygone Days
'The Beast Book' ('Sefer habehemot')
   8
*Be'emek habakhah see In the Valley of
   Tears*
The Beggar Book (*Sefer hakabtzanim*)
   Reb Alter   62, 63, 87, 92–3
   beggars in 17–19; Jews as species of
      59
   and Mendele's other works   18
   Feibush   96
   Fishke the Lame   18, 74
   Jews as alien to natural world in
      76–7
   as love story   18
   and Mendele (author): personal
      knowledge of beggars   5, 28, 33,
      90–1

and Mendele (fictional character)   16,
   31; ambivalence to Jews 107; anger
   at communal authorities 43; family
   40; as orthodox Jew 33; sensitivity
   to projection 106; sidelock cut by
   antisemite 34
   starvation in   85
   'twin Mendeles'   44
   wagon scene in   62, 63
Belinsky, Vissarion   5, 53
'Beseter ra'am *see* 'Shelter from the
   Storm'
Bialik, Chaim Nachman   3, 10, 38,
   87 n., 89
bias
   psychology of 58, 106
   in Russian Hebrew literature   51
   see also antisemitism; Jews, stereotypes
   and images in Mendele; Mendele
   Mocher Sefarim, life, and Jewish
   self-hate
Bible, the   14, 15, 16–17, 19, 20, 23,
   26, 40, 47, 64, 66, 79, 83, 99, 100,
   111
Binstock, Judah Leib   9, 90, 105, 113
'Biyemei hara'ash *see* 'Earthquake Days'
'Biyeshivah shel ma'alah uviyeshivah shel
   matah' *see* 'Warsaw 1881'
Blake, William   96
Braudes, Reuben Asher   113 n.
Brill, Joseph   51, 113 n.

'The Calf'
   appalling good health of Jewish boy
      in   61–2
   description of good teacher in   93
   drafts of   8
   motif of loss of father in   87
   nightmare of slaughter, compared with
      Chaplin   29–30, 61–2, 87, 93
censorship, in Russia   6, 49, 104

Printed and bound by CPI Group (UK) Ltd, Croydon, CR0 4YY

13/04/2025